HEART OF SHADOWS
(LORD BYRON AND THE SUPERNATURAL)

by

Derek Fox and Mike Vardy

Blackie & Co Publishers Ltd

BLACKIE & CO PUBLISHERS LIMITED
PAPERBACK

A CIP catalogue record for this title is available from the British
Library ISBN 1 903 138 01 9

Blackie & Co Publishers Limited
www.blackiepublishers.com

Photographs for cover and interior by Mike Vardy
Email:
mike.photos@virgin.net<mailto:mike.photos@virgin.net

Cover Design by Creative Identity
Email: fred@creative-identity.com

Printed and bound in Gt Britain

For Kath and Sallie 'Devoted in the stormiest hour.'

DEREK FOX   MIKE VARDY

DETAIL FROM THOMAS PHILLIPS PORTRAIT OF
LORD BYRON (1814)
BY KIND PERMISSION OF
CITY OF NOTTINGHAM MUSEUMS,
NEWSTEAD ABBEY

ACKNOWLEDGEMENTS

Grateful thanks to Brian Ayers, the Custodian at Newstead Abbey, whose support and co-operation proved invaluable. Thanks also to Housekeeper Maisie Hammond who was instrumental in bringing us and the Abbey together. We also appreciate the time spared by the numerous guides who gave their time to relate, in their own inimitable way, their experiences over their years of working there.

In no specific order of priority these are Patricia Davis ('Trish'); Barbara Holton (whose terrifying confrontation with the Black Friar really made us shiver); Susan Patching; Ray Hadley (Stay clear of creaking stairs, Ray!), and Pauline Corby who had rather an unusual plane journey. Thanks also to Christine Davies who had her hair reshaped, John Concannon who, at the time of writing still awaits sight of the 'big dog' about whom he warns visitors. Not least is Jill Tanner, who children on school visits to the Abbey know as 'Mrs. Emelia Webb'.

Because Newstead is such a populated place, several other guides about whose experiences we were informed deserve recognition. Our thanks are therefore conveyed to Audrey, Wendy, Angela, Jane, Elizabeth, Georgina and Enid, some of whom have left the Abbey, although we're unsure why (?)

Further appreciation is due the management and staff of the White Lady Restaurant, namely: Maureen Crisp and Ken Purslow who kindly directed us to speak to Christine Marrison and Mark Milburn who, in addition to their own weird experiences, also related the disturbing events that beset part-time waitresses Linda Kershaw and Sarah Anderson.

We acknowledge the kind co-operation of Archivist, Haidee Jackson, who allowed access to Newstead's archives. Also Dennis G Hill, who directed us to audio tapes containing accounts from several former employees over the years. These include the late Edie Barker whose relatives we were unable to contact. We trust they will welcome seeing their names and experiences in print, wherever they happen to reside.

Thank you especially to Bettina Croft and all at Blackie for having faith in the project.

Penultimately, grateful thanks are extended to our wives, Kath and Sallie, who literally became 'Ghost Widows' while the book was being written. Kindred spirits? We believe so.

Of course the greatest acknowledgement is due to Lord Byron, his home, Newstead Abbey and naturally the other 'occupants' who we believe gave their approval in order to see their own experiences in print.

Derek Fox
Mike Vardy
December, 2000

FOREWORD

It is an impossible task for any one book, be it narrative or painstaking biography, to illuminate every facet of the life of a genius. 'Heart of Shadows' - well reasearched as it is - makes no claim to be a definitive biography. Its authors light a candle and lead us through the portals of Newstead Abbey, Byron's ancestral home. We are shown the dark forces of heredity and history which influenced so much of his life and work.

This book is but one more window through which we are invited to observe and perhaps come to understand the tortured mind of a supremely gifted yet ultimately self-destructive man. As I turned the pages, I was able once again to see, touch and absorb the very essence of the Abbey which had so affected me when I visited some years ago.

Byron's travels took him across Europe, eventually to Greece, where he gave his wealth and health to the cause of Greek independence. Finally, his weakened constitution succumbed to fever and death in Messolongi. Even then, the ghosts of Newstead reached out to claim his restless soul. His genius lives on, an inspiration to scholar and romantic alike. I like to believe that his heart remains here in the sunshine of Greece, buried beneath his monument in the Garden of Heroes. But perhaps his spirit does return to the grey walls and perfumed gardens of the only home he really loved, Newstead Abbey.

Ioannis Manessi
Athens, November 2000

CHAPTER ONE

DARKNESS

--oOo--

I

'And the clouds perish'd! Darkness had no need
Of aid from them - She was the universe.'

A solitary man, bereft of friends and acquaintances, his mind focussed on the past, sits isolated in the dark, forbidding confines of his home.

He warms himself by a lonely fire, shapes from dark corners quickened by flickering candlelight: his own imagination torments, the very stones prompting nebulous shapes to remain...victimise...

Voices of his ancestors call...are linked to his *now*, and perhaps his future. An embellished silver skull cup, fashioned from the head of a long dead, disinterred prior, sits before him, stained red by...firelight? Wine?

An unseen watcher entices him down cheerless corridors into and through desolate, despairing rooms. It leads him towards darker depths where, in that curious half-world which only true genius can inhabit, he is finally able to grasp its essence.

Is this building, this place he once looked upon as home, ensnaring him, bidding him remain...in whatever form?

Time distorts the mind; it eventually urges recollections. This man is hardly alone in this, and must reflect on his past before he can ever achieve a new future.

II

On an autumn day in 1798, three passengers - Mother, Nurse and a ten-year old, slightly lame boy - nervously alight from a coach at Newstead Toll Bar. Excited, and relieved at completing an arduous journey, they ask the Toll-Keeper in jest if there happens to be a nobleman's estate nearby.

The Keeper nods towards two miserable wooden gates. "It used to be Lord Byron's, but he is dead."

"So who owns it now?" The mother asks.

"Why, it is owned by a little boy in Aberdeen."

"And this is him," cries a proud nurse, "God bless him!" She gives the boy a lingering kiss.

'Mrs Gordon's crooked devil', so named by Aberdeen stall holders because of mischievous pranks he played upon them, had come to claim his inheritance.

He was the only son of 'Mad' Jack Byron and Catherine, daughter of George Gordon of Gight and Catherine Innes of Rosieburn. Defying superstition, Catherine married Jack on the thirteenth day of the month, and despite these connotations, ensuing years would see her son capture the imagination of generations, become lover to famous ladies of his time, and perhaps the most celebrated poet in English literature.

Born on the 22nd January 1788, George Gordon Noel Byron, in his eleventh year, succeeds to the Byron family title becoming the 6th Lord. In the spring of 1798, seven years after his father's death, Catherine is informed of the demise of the 5th Lord, and spends the following summer preparing for the journey from Scotland to Nottinghamshire.

Anticipating a future lifestyle in a resplendent mansion populated by liveried servants, they were met with the expenses of the 5th Lord's funeral, and a decrepit pile of stone, which had once been a home. With little money left after meeting travel expenses; with no possibility of retracing their steps, they hesitate beneath the Pilgrim Oak, nervous at the prospect of journeying through a bleak, treeless landscape raped by the poet's dissolute predecessor.

The resulting disenchantment of the young Byron's first view of his inheritance doubtless prompted the following verses:

'Through thy battlements, Newstead,
the hollow winds whistle;
Thou, the hall of my fathers, art gone to decay;
In thy once smiling garden the hemlock and thistle
Have choked up the rose which bloomed by the
way.'

'Newstead! What saddening sense of change is thine,
Thy yawning arch betokens sure decay;
The last and youngest of a noble line

Now holds thy mouldering turrets in his sway.
'Deserted now he scans the grey-worn towers,
Thy vaults where dead of feudal ages sleep,
Thy cloisters, pervious to the winter showers,
These - these he views, and views them but to weep.'

A forlorn, ivy encrusted facade, its dark, leaded lights painted on the lake's surface; the bankrupted West Front's priory church craving assistance of a heaven that had perhaps forsaken it. Derelict and empty apart from a handful of miserable retainers, the boy remains in awe of its decadent grandeur. His cries of glee are swallowed by a distorted carillon of rooks wheeling and crying, reminiscent of the disembodied souls of ancient canons still refusing to relinquish their hold on a once sanctified pile.

Therefore, do other unseen, yet expectant eyes note the young Lord's arrival, ready to greet this new incumbent, welcome him to the fold?

Devil Byron's angst still clings, his unabated fury increased by the realisation that his successor would be the grandson of his hated brother, Admiral The Hon. John Byron.

III

William, the 5th Lord, known as the Wicked Lord, or *Devil Byron*, inherited Newstead Priory in 1736.

On the 28th March 1747 and only eighteen, Elizabeth Shaw became Lady Byron. The only daughter and heiress of Charles Shaw of Besthorpe Park, Norfolk, her fortune of £70,000 was soon squandered by her ne'er do well husband.

Eighteen years on, and after a drunken duel in the shadowed room of a London tavern, this wild, dissolute Byron killed his neighbour, William Chaworth of Annesley, and subsequently sought permanent anonymity at Newstead. Increasing dementia was visited on family, servants and estates alike, this degeneracy knowing no bounds.

On one occasion, enraged, he cast his wife, Elizabeth, into a pond. On another, he shot his coachman, threw his corpse into the carriage already occupied by Lady Byron and, taking the reins, whipped up the frightened animals and drove off in a frenzy. Subsequently, he disposed of several other estates, blatantly ignored his family and often quarrelled with neighbours and contemporaries.

A *strange* individual, he had the knack of antagonising all around him. In 1771, he introduced an additional boat to his already established 'navy' which included a twenty-gun ship maintained on the Upper Lake at Newstead. Legend has it that local people filled this 'new' boat with heather, or *ling,* as it journeyed through Sherwood Forest bound for the Abbey in the hope that the prophecy of Yorkshire witch, Mother Shipton, would be fulfilled and Newstead would be lost to the Byrons.

His odd nautical obsession is evidenced by the two forts on the Upper Lake; yet one other of Devil Byron's structures - *Folly Castle* - being dismantled in the late 19th century. Built just beyond the Upper Lake and reputed to be the scene of unspeakable orgies, even decades after its demolition, Folly Castle's tainted ground is still considered to be haunted.

In 1772, during one of his absences from Newstead, he ordered the Eagle Pond to be drained, the operation said to reveal a brass eagle lectern and two candlesticks hidden by the canons prior to the Abbey's Dissolution in 1539. Rumour is also rife that the mud held two treasure chests but prior to any salvage operation, an urgent message 'to refill the pond at once' came from Byron, who was expecting guests. Obviously, he was clearly unaware of the bounty he may have been casting aside, given his straitened circumstances, yet the fearful servants obeyed his missive without question, desperate to complete the task before he arrived.

No-one dared reveal what had been lost, and as far as is known these chests still remain unrecovered.

Eventually, Byron converted the lectern and candlesticks into much needed cash, selling them to Sir Richard Kaye (later Dean of Lincoln and Archdeacon of Nottingham).

The hollow lectern pedestal ostensibly contained a number of parchment deeds and grants bearing the seals of Edward III and Henry VIII. Amongst these was an indulgence granted to the canons in which plenary pardon was assured in advance for some months for all kinds of crimes. Several of the most gross and sensual are specifically mentioned.

Not surprisingly, Byron's deplorable eccentricities resulted in his marriage to Elizabeth foundering and effectively ending in 1778.

Violent mood swings caused him to shun his hitherto favoured sister after her marriage to a gamekeeper, who

Byron had deemed unsuitable. Convinced Byron would forgive her, she determined to intercept him on his way home but he ignored her and galloped on. Her cries of desperation still ring out, for every year on a late autumn day when the leaves fly, and the park is a myriad of light and shade, an unseen horse is heard galloping through the park to the plaintive accompaniment of: *'Speak to me, my Lord Byron, only speak to me!'*

'I fear them not, and feel for thee alone -
Speak to me! Though it be in wrath...'

ONE OF THE "OLD LORD'S DEVILS"

In October 1784, undaunted by these traumas, he erected statues of a male and a female satyr in Newstead's grounds in an area that became known as Devil's Wood. Because of their diabolical attributes, such as horns and cloven feet, the locals believed them to be the object of some secret rite and christened them *'the Old Lord's devils'*. So the 'Wicked Lord' won the unsavoury accolade of Devil Byron, whose statues now leer from the terrace across the Eagle Pond, a chilling memorial to his wayward lifestyle.

Shortage of money promoted further desperate measures including the sale of Newstead's priceless collections and practically denuding the park of trees, one notable exception being the *Pilgrim Oak*. For centuries pilgrims would take respite beneath it before entering the Priory's religious sanctuary.

This tree was looked upon as sacred and mystical, revered by locals who would gather on holidays and feast days to celebrate their rural festivals. Determined to protect the oak and despite their crushing poverty, they *ransomed* their sacred tree from the *Devil*.

Worsening financial straits forced Byron to order that the Abbey's interior be stripped. In 1779, he suggested to Daws, his steward, that *'a little money might be maid* [sic] *from the inside of Newstead, such as Chimney Pieces Brass locks flooring Wenscote &c: &c:, tho I cant Pull down the House I have power to sell all materials in the inside also the Game...'*

A curious entry appears in the accounts for October of that year: *'Paid William Bell for searching in the cloisters, etc., at Newstead for a vault or cellar, etc., 14s.6d.'*

Fifty years on, the 6th Lord's former housekeeper, Nanny Smith, when recounting certain of her experiences to Washington Irving, the American author, would refer to the cloister flags being lifted to reveal the bones of dead canons sealed in stone coffins.

With life, lands and home deteriorating, the flow of visitors ceased as Devil Byron's behaviour became more erratic. Stories and superstitions grew; servants departed for other employment; tenants, unsure of their reception, approached with growing trepidation, Devil Byron's only companions being Joe Murray who assisted him with his 'navy', and Elizabeth Hardstaff, 'housekeeper', whose relationship with his lordship went beyond that of master and servant. This earned Elizabeth the nickname of 'Lady Betty'.

The 5th Lord's sad end came on the 21st May 1798. In abject misery, living practically alone in the only room in the house left weatherproof, his solitary distraction was to feed crickets that abounded in the household. They were said to recognise his voice and appear when he called. On the night he died, one of the few who dared visit him, on passing through the Great Hall, heard a chirping sound. Looking down he observed a horde of crickets departing through the open door never to be seen again!

This wealth of emotive legends surrounding the Wicked 5th Lord, has granted him his place amidst the unrequited dead, his restless spirit welcomed to their ranks... In the loosest sense, he died without issue, five children and a grandson having pre-deceased him, what remained passing to *'the penniless little boy in Aberdeen...'*

IV

For weeks, young George Gordon revelled in and explored every corner of his ravaged home. Untroubled, the boy enjoyed befriending his tenants, his attention welcomed by all in contrast to the oppression they had hitherto suffered at the hands of the *Devil*.

'I have so much endured - so much endured - Look on me! The grave hath not changed thee more Than I am changed for thee.'

Byron stares at sad, seeping walls and wonders aloud, "What secrets do you hold? Damn you, what secrets will you share with me, a disheartened poet whose lines, though placed on paper, are lines which mirror my heart...my soul?

" Newstead, I damn you, love you. Why then do you not speak to me, as my damnable forebear's sister demanded he speak to her?"

He drinks from the cup, one bottle of claret becoming slowly depleted, his mind given over to more fanciful imaginings. He mutters: "Aye, what *will* you share with me?"

Ears attuned, he listens. "What are you whispering? I can't...yes. But do I really wish to know?"

Times past, present and future? Whatever, times remembered. "Indeed, past events, *my past*, have a habit of promoting future happenings. I remain enamoured, but afraid." From dark eyes the depths of his soul surface. *"'We are eternal; and to us the past is, as the future, present.'* Thus, what part will you play in my life?" His voice falters, one thought retained: *And in my death?*

Words that would later appear in a letter he would write on 20th August 1821 to his publisher, John Murray. *'I am not sure that long life is desirable for one of my temper and constitutional depression of Spirits...It has been deepened perhaps by some long past events...You know, or do you not know, that my maternal Grandfather...was strongly suspected of Suicide...and that another very near relative of the same branch took poison...'*

His features appear gaunt, troubled. "So, dear God, what of the future?"

He stares about him. "Oh, I see you all there gathered in the gloom, reminding me of what was and is yet to come."

A tapestry swirls in the draught through a rotted casement. A disdainful laugh. Him, or perhaps something else?

"Ghosts?" He rises, the chair tilts, to fall back again, hardly noticed amidst a multitude of other sounds. Voices: in the air, in the whole fabric of the house he still calls home.

"Yes, I acknowledge you: Father, great grandfather, uncle this, uncle that...And you, dim figure, skulking in deeper shades, who are you? What part do you play in the game?"

A profound silence falls, the fire crackles, sparks cascade up the wide chimney. No-one answers.

"Ah, to hell, restless shade." He turns again. "So, great grandfather, what is it you desire? Come to claim me?" His laugh is cold, echoes in the stillness. "Oh no, sir, I feel not yet... hardly yet. I still have a destiny to fulfil. A welter of past demands it." He ruminates awhile, sips again from the cup. "Aye, and there's a question: What past? How much?"

The chair creaks as he sits and refills the skull cup. The wine has an effect, his eyes cloud; they dim...

He awakes to a shaft of sunlight angled through the high casement. Rising stiffly, he stretches, head pounding from a surfeit of wine. At the window, he opens the catch, aware suddenly of the heady scent of flowers and subdued voices. He looks out...

CHAPTER TWO

FOUNDATIONS

--oOo--

I

SPANISH GARDEN - A PLACE OF QUIET
CONTEMPLATION

He sees...

Black habits drifting amongst colourful gardens, the Canons Regular of St. Augustine undertaking daily chores, enjoying leisure time walking, relishing the gardens they had painstakingly laid out. It is summer, these gardens, hemmed in by yew hedges, a source of produce and pleasure - a place of quiet contemplation and gentle dispute amidst the heady scent of flowers.

This essence hangs in the air, is absorbed into the very fabric of the building, prompting in Byron painful memories of a mother both loved and despised. He repeats quietly, "...*I have brought you a shawl, and a quantity of Attar [sic] of Roses, but these I must smuggle if possible.*"

Remembered lines penned to his mother during his journey home after spending two years travelling through Greece, returning on the frigate *Volgate* to arrive in Portsmouth, England on the 4th July 1811.

Sadly, Byron never sees his mother again. She dies on the 1st August before he can reach Newstead and present her with a favourite perfume: thoughts too overwhelming to contemplate... yet.

Turning from the window, he looks upon the figure still sleeping, his dream shade melding back into his physical self.

A noise, noises, hard to define at first, rising to a scream, becoming an intrusive terror. He jerks awake, the fire smoulders, the wine cup half full, his white-knuckled hands grip the arms of the great chair. "Where do you lead me now?"

As though possessed, he rises from the chair, another nearly full bottle clenched in his hand. The stones cajole, whispers lure him through the Cloisters, to pass unseen by huddled groups of monks enjoying their leisure amidst a rattle of counters, the chink of coins, impervious to the ranting, still distant screams.

As a die is cast, Byron, a fish snared by an invisible thread, is reeled along against his will, his curiosity forcing him to mount the stone staircase thence through the Great Hall, booted feet stirring even more echoes. Damp ceilings and crumbled coving throw out the piercing cries of an animal in pain.

A narrow, curving stair, muted light from a solitary, stained glass window - he knows this route and treads lightly on the steps, the bottle he carries chinking against stone. Everything is familiar, even the door beyond, leading to his own dressing room. He pushes the door...

Onto a scattering of rude litters, of monks garbed in black habits, muttering, groaning in their pain. A malodorous stench of sickness and soiled clothing pervades, yet it is hardly this that causes him to baulk.

The screams die, muffled by the work-worn hand of a cloaked figure occupying the shadows, beyond it the pale, emaciated shape of a young boy, lifeless and naked, carelessly flung onto a pile of sacks in a dim corner.

The brother turns towards Byron...He has no face! Nothing recognisable exists beneath the miserable cowl.

Byron spins abruptly, hoping to escape the apparition. In the opposite corner he sees a number of people including two women, apparently agitated. The women are dressed in shorter skirts, their lower limbs visible. Such apparel is alien to him, and he remains transfixed, staring in disbelief at one, whose face seems repulsed by something she has witnessed. Dizzy, he stumbles, the bottle shatters: wine, like blood, spreads in an ever-widening stain as he curls foetus-like in the centre of the Oratory floor.

Strange voices assail him, their language very different from his own. They come from the adjoining room - his bedroom?

"My name is Maisie Hammond. I started working here on the 21st May 1984."

Byron is perplexed. What date is this? It is impossible!

Conscience intrudes: Come, my lord, in your own words you state '...to us the past is, as the future, present...' Do not forget that you looked out of the window and saw the monks. What date did you consider that to be?

"'Tis a dream. I *am* influenced by alcohol, and perhaps the essence of this place."

You asked the question, m'lord, so by whose right do you question the intentions of those who seek to enlighten you? Listen. And learn.

Maisie's voice echoes from the present. "One of the two women was a medium from Leicester, brought to Newstead Abbey by the producers of an American television series on 'Ghosts in Stately Homes.' The woman came into the Oratory but didn't stay very long. Her face was like putty, you could tell she was distressed, even afraid.

"But the TV people wanted more so, prompted by her daughter who agreed to accompany her, the woman reluctantly returned to the room, the two of them sitting together. The woman quickly became distraught. Unable to control herself she ran back in here.

"Naturally, I was concerned and did overhear the woman telling her daughter what she had experienced in the Oratory.

"'I felt as if there were a child present', the woman said in a faltering tone, 'but one that goes way back in history. He was either extremely ill, you know in pain, or was being tortured, I'm not quite sure.'"

"Why then should she become victim to such extreme reaction, I asked myself," Maisie continues. She answers her own question. "Perhaps, on reflection, her gift of second sight was the catalyst. Maybe it exposed some of this place's darker secrets, secrets it wants to retain. Whatever, the woman found this revelation so traumatic she felt compelled to flee the building."

"Let me quote Byron here: *'Tis said thou holdest converse with the things which are forbidden to the search of man; that with the dwellers of the dark abodes, the many evil and unheavenly spirits which walk the valley of the shade of death, thou communest.'*

"As I said, it was a child, but so far back. They would be training young boys here when it was a religious order. For four hundred years it was a monastic building."

"It is true that religious houses regularly trained boys as secular clerks," interjects a male voice. "It did release them from a possible lifetime of grinding poverty." He pauses before adding speculatively, "Yet at what price?"

II

The Canons Regular of St. Augustine, the Black Canons-derived from the black habits they wore - came to the district in 1170, there to establish a holy order in the place named 'New Steade' or *new place*, its first recorded dwelling being a timber-framed house.

Ostensibly, the order lived a very frugal, pious life, but did they lead such an incorruptible existence? Certainly they did not live a life of total abstinence, several being amongst the first inhabitants of Newstead to wallow in delectations of the flesh.

In 1266-79, Archbishop Gifford ordered the Prior to foster more love for his brethren rather than be feared by them, take more care of the brethren in the Infirmary and forbade excessive drinking and 'inordinate roaming in the fields'. In July, 1280, he ordered that Robert of Hickling and John of Tickhill be punished for the benefit of their morals and on the 11th January 1286, the sacrist was ordered to restore a loan of 20 marks made by William of Markeaton by Christmas, charged him with insolence to his brethren and forbade the game of dice. In 1314, Thomas of Burton, a canon, was implicated in serious excess.

Seven years earlier, in 1307, Archbishop Greenfield visited Newstead and found the Prior accused of 'incontinence' with Emma of Quernley and Emma of Papplewick. On the 27th January 1308, he appointed a Commissioner to receive the Prior's purgation along with several other canons. The implication is impossible to avoid. In a world where religion and superstition went hand in hand, where those who practised both were feared, where their morals went unquestioned, the opportunity to conceal often unspeakable conduct was readily available.

The Priory's transition from religious to country house is echoed by Byron:

'Years roll on years; to ages, ages yield;
Abbots to abbots, in a line, succeed;
Religion's character their protecting shield,
Till royal sacrilege, their doom decreed.

'One holy Henry rear'd the Gothic walls,
And bade the pious inmates rest in peace;
Another Henry the kind gift recalls,
And bids devotion's hallow'd echoes cease.'

In 1539, Henry VIII ordered the Dissolution thus ending a regime which could be both secretive and arbitrary, and capable of harsh, outrageous practices.

Amongst many to bear Henry's wrath was Newstead Priory, which one year later passed into the keeping of Sir John Byron who oversaw the Dissolution. The Deed of Suppression was signed by the Prior, Robert Blake, the Sub-Prior, the Cellarer and nine other canons, though legend has it that the Dissolution was far from peaceful, with those who resisted Henry's terms either turned away penniless, tortured, imprisoned, or slain.

In deference to Byron's lines, were the canons so devoted inasmuch as John Landon, King Henry VIII's Commissioner had previously advised them... *'to torn som of ther seremonyns of ydilnes unto som bodely exercise, and nott to sytt all day lurking in the cloisters ydellye.'?*

If not, then what has been their legacy?

The air is displaced by the swish of fabric. Byron's eyes flicker, he recoils, confronted, and appalled by a shape blocking out all light. It wears the same coarse fabric and exudes the same threatening aspect as that already witnessed The coarseness caresses Byron's cheek; then there is nothing. Vision only slightly impaired, he ponders what he has seen.

Imagination? Perhaps a fancy stemming from idleness, the need to do something other than reside in this vast, echoing hall of his fathers.

The damning word *idle* lingers despite the insufferable headache brought on by a surfeit of wine. He rises, his gaze transfixed by the stain, so reminiscent of a foetus in the womb.

"Is this me, not yet born?" He wonders aloud. "Or is it merely proof that I still remain here 'in the form of my birth...reappeared to the day'?"

He paces. Past indiscretion walks with him. "Was I idle, along with my cronies when, in my inveterate youth I sought refuge in high living and wenching? Is this, I wonder, my torture? The deadliest sin to love as we have loved."

Pistol cracks ricochet from the past: he lurches downstairs, the beginnings of a smile taunting his lips.

There they all are in the Great Hall. He joins them.

As he steps through the door a pistol ball whistles within a hair's breadth of his face so close he can feel it, a chunk of plaster blasted from the wall nearby.

"Have a care," he shouts, "there are enough ghosts here without my adding to their number!"

Charles Skinner Matthews roars with laughter. "We have a care, m'lord? Come, it is we who should be cautious. I imparted to the others on our journey here: *'...Have a care how you proceed...Be mindful to go there in broad daylight, and with your eyes about you; for should you make any blunder - should you go to the right of the hall steps, you are laid hold of by a bear; and should you go to the left your case is still worse, for you run full against a wolf!'*

Byron accepts this with humour. "Aye, and once past them we court the dangers of our own making." He turns to Scrope Davies and whispers, *"'...I have no objection to an occasional sacrifice to Momus, or even deities of a less harmful description-...'"* He laughs. "Always it is so. Even this dilapidation fails to prevent you and your *'bevy of inmates'* from banging away at one end of this stricken room with your pistols. Ironically, *'...there is something Pagan in me that I cannot shake off...'"*

And he realises well enough that once the gauntlet has been run, and the individual welcomed, the real partying will commence.

Carousing, indulging in Bacchanalian games with the opposite sex, keeping his dogs in the chapel, and using the mortuary crypt as a swimming bath became orders of the day, any day!

"So what do we partake of this day," Byron inquires. "Do we ride, box, fence; continue our practice with pistols? Or -" He tenders a malign grin. "Or do we play with the bear and the wolf, if someone would be so good and brave as to loose their chains?

"No? Cowards all then. You have run the gauntlet, and now refuse to renew their acquaintance. Come gentlemen, you all know where they lounge, it is merely a matter of loosening either one or t'other, or both, from by the front door on the south side of the house."

His words meet little resistance as he again views an empty room, his sigh reluctant to follow as he departs, mind courting pleasant enough memories.

Downstairs, another barren, low-ceilinged room with a Gothic vaulted roof, remains cold and empty where once it was charged with laughter and drunken carousing.

The skull cup taunts from the table. In a time where dark humour enabled baiting of his contemporaries, the night hours would lead them into less wholesome pursuits.

'The Order of the Skull' - at its centre the embellished silver skull cup, the once proud head of a resurrected prior - had been established as a means of further recreation. The clique numbered thirteen with Byron as Abbot. The twelve others included his good friends Mathews, Hobhouse, Wedderburn and Webster, and Scrope Davies.

He recollects how: "We went down to Newstead together, where I had got a famous cellar, and *Monks'* dresses from a famous masquerade warehouse..."

Dressed in monastic garb, they recited verse and drank into the night from the brimming, wine filled cup formed from a skull Byron himself discovered whilst walking in the garden.

Regarding this, he told Thomas Medwin, *'A strange fancy seized me of having it mounted as a drinking cup. I accordingly sent it to town and it was turned with a very high polish, and of a mottled colour of a tortoise shell.'*

His lips move silently reciting further lines underscored by his droll drinking humour:

> *'Start not, nor deem my spirit fled:*
> *In me behold the only skull.*
> *From which, unlike the living head,*
> *Whatever flows is never dull.'*

THE ORDER OF THE SKULL

Bouts of lust and revelry with housemaids and married women of questionable morals followed. Indeed one of his maidservants, Lucy, fell pregnant and eventually bore him a son. Whilst apparently not in love with the girl, Byron did bestow his generosity upon her by making her an allowance of £50 per annum, plus a similar amount to the child.

Matthews, a ringleader in this unwholesome, male orientated foolery, always called Byron 'the Abbot', and often played the *ghost!*

The fire dies, a warm body extricates itself from Byron. He reaches out only to touch cold air. Past and present become two sides of a flag, close yet only distinguishable from the angle at which they are viewed.

His present is lonely, filled with still sought after images behind closed lids...

Cooling ash in the grate, wanton revelry done, Byron, eyes and mind dulled through excess, contemplates his friends. The room is dim, lamps splutter and die, visibility curtailed. He plays his own game, determined to count them as they either sit, lie or loll against walls, the room resonant with their snores and mutterings.

"Aye, there's Hobhouse, chin on chest, dribbling as usual, ruining another shirt. And Matthews slumped by the window breathing like a bellows. Damn, if only Matthews hadn't denied playing the trick..."

Hobhouse had stumbled through the door, an extinguished candle in his hand shouting at Matthews.

"Villain, sir, you very nearly stopped my heart with your tricks!"

Matthews, a little worse for wear, had disentangled himself from voluptuous curves looking perplexed. "Come, Hobhouse, what tricks?"

"Why, rising out of the great stone coffin as you did and snuffing out my light."

Matthews and Byron exchange glances, a somewhat bemused, startled grin on their faces.

"But John," Matthews protests, "this sylph will testify I have most recently been 'otherwise engaged' in her welcoming embrace."

Hobhouse stutters and mumbles, "Perhaps too much wine." He flops into a vacant chair. Still stupefied, Byron is alerted by this exchange and recommences counting his cronies. "Fourteen. The Order is all present."

He jerks upright, his head heavy. *"Fourteen?"* Impossible. The Order is but thirteen. "So who makes jest by dressing in old fashioned Cavalier raiment?"

He jabs the air. "You, sir, why are you not dressed in clothes befitting the occasion?"

Ah, it is no jest my lord, merely history. All part of your ancestry.

III

In 1640, Sir John Byron purchased Newstead for the sum of £800. Ownership subsequently passed to his son, Little Sir John Byron of the Great Beard, under whose care the house prospered. A man of learning, so attached was Little Sir John to Newstead that, over ensuing years, he has often been seen to step down from his portrait and seat himself at a table in the Library where he proceeds to pore over his precious books.

The original grant of 1640 still hangs in the Abbey.

The Byron family's varied, often illustrious history, is closely bound to Newstead and its environs, none more notable than the seven brothers who rallied behind the banner of King Charles I during the English Civil Wars from 1642 to 1649, some giving their lives in its ferocious campaigns.

After months spent with King and Parliament jockeying for position, the English Civil Wars began at six o' clock on the evening of 22nd August 1642 when, in the teeth of a gale, Charles I raised his standard at Nottingham on Standard Hill just below the castle. That night the wind tore down the standard, this event considered by most to be an ill omen.

The Country rapidly descended into a conflagration that carved a swathe through the male populous and pitched brother against brother. In the Byrons' case, however, all seven brothers were staunchly Royalist. They fought for Charles at the Battle of Marston Moor and eventually three of them, Thomas, Philip and Nicholas, lost their lives, sometimes in vainglorious circumstances. A fourth brother, Sir William, disappeared, presumed killed in the fighting. This prompted the 6th Lord to paint a florid, yet somewhat inaccurate portrait of their exploits:

'On Marston Moor, with Rupert 'gainst traitors
contending,
Four brothers enrich'd with blood the bleak field,
For the rights of a monarch, their country defending,
Till death their attachment to royalty seal'd.'

The death toll at major set-pieces varied. At some it was surprisingly light, others nothing less than a massacre. With conflicting bands of Royalists and Parliamentarians roaming the countryside, many lives were lost in minor skirmishes such as the Battle of East Stoke in the Trent Valley, scant distance from Newstead.

Nearby Newark did hold out as a Royalist stronghold for virtually the entire war, but Nottingham, despite being the place where the whole murderous episode became ignited, was basically for Parliament. When Charles and his forces moved out it quickly declared its allegiances, and became the site of many bloody skirmishes in ensuing years.

Occupied by Royalists, Newstead, along with nearby Felley Priory and Kirkby Hardwick, inevitably became embroiled in conflict. On the 10th January 1644, war finally visited when Parliamentary cavalry from Nottinghamshire and Derbyshire, together with three Yorkshire regiments, assembled at nearby Mansfield and set out to storm these manor houses.

Details are sketchy. Certainly Newstead was besieged but it was short-lived, the garrison there quickly surrendering. Never conceived as a fortress, the Abbey would be impossible to defend over any length of time. Surprisingly none of the Byron brothers died in the attack, all apparently campaigning elsewhere.

Nor do we know if any other lives were lost, although it is possible. In the totality of casualties generated by the Civil War, an odd life or two lost in an inconsequential encounter became insignificant. Musket balls had peppered Newstead's stonework - a sign of a particularly sharp encounter? Or merely trigger-happy marksmen using the crumbling West Front for target practice, aiming at the statues adorning it? Tradition promotes that divine intervention prevented their rounds hitting the statue of the Virgin and Child sited at the apex, the Virgin Mary being the patron saint of the Priory.

Byron's imagination again comes to the fore:

'An abbey once, a regal fortress now,
Encircled by insulting rebel powers,
War's dread machines o'erhanging thy threatn'ing brow,
And dart destruction in sulphurous showers.

Ah, vain defence! The hostile traitor's siege,
Though oft repulsed, by guile o'ercomes the brave;
His thronging foes oppress the faithful liege,
Rebellion's reeking standards o'er him wave.

*****

There many a pale and ruthless robber's corse,
Noisesome and aghast, defiles thy sacred sod;
O'ermingling man, the horse commix'd with horse,
Corruption's heap, the savage spoilers trod.'

Lives were lost when a wagon train carrying booty from Newstead came under attack from a one-hundred strong force of Royalist cavalry from Wingfield Manor in Derbyshire, under the command of Sir John Frecheville. The Royalists laid siege to the wagons near Bestwood Park, but were repulsed leaving seven of their number dead, others wounded.

Despite the spirited efforts of the Royalists, Parliament gradually gained mastery. An interesting anecdote emphasising this ascendancy is that in 1648 Oliver Cromwell slept at Newstead on his way to fight at Preston. Even more ironic - following his failure to take North Wales for the King that same year - the eldest of the seven Byron brothers, yet another Sir John, spent his last four years in Holland in pitiful exile without possibility of pardon from Parliament.

Exile, imposed or self-imposed, would become a feature of the Byron family.

So, my lord, who is this fourteenth, uninvited guest?

Is it Sir John finally returned from exile? Or some unknown unfortunate who perished for his beliefs risen from '*One red burial blount*', that mass grave of Royalist dead discovered close by, whose occupants were not buried in the Christian manner, east to west, but lying with their faces turned towards the east in unquiet sleep?

Neither should we dismiss the actions undertaken on the 15th January 1644, when a force of Royalists caught the Nottingham garrison by surprise. The Parliamentary forces re-grouped to prevent the Royalists taking control of the city, even though it took days of bitter, house-to-house fighting to dislodge the occupying forces. Many died and many more were seriously wounded. Once they had cleared the city, Cromwell's troops pursued those they had dislodged across fields and through woods, the fugitives leaving a ghastly trail of wounded. Starved with the bitter cold, most bled to death within their wooded sanctuary.

Could it therefore be the shade of an unfortunate - from whichever encounter - who now haunts the woods surrounding Newstead, and who appeared to a boy playing Hide and Seek, a child who ran ashen-faced to his friends, terrified of the man dressed in dated soldier's apparel.

If he visits with you now, my lord, then what of the future, beyond even yourself? Who might see him then?

These terrible times appear to have left more than one indelible stain on the Abbey, not least in the room adopted as a bedroom by a Byron successor to the property, Emilia Webb.

A sombre place, the room's dark oak panelling around walls and across the ceiling, drains the room of natural light and encourages its foreboding atmosphere. Over the years servants have avoided this room complaining that a column of cold, white vapour emanates from its floor's centre in the dead of night.

Emilia Webb discounted such phenomena and remains one individual who must count herself fortunate, for the 'apparition' has *not* gone away. In recent years, Christine Davies, an Abbey guide, climbed the stairs in the South East Wing to find the door to the Webbs' bedroom open, the aperture filled with what appeared to be white smoke. Alarmed that the room might be on fire, she recklessly dashed forward to quell the blaze only to find the room unscathed.

In 1994, following a well-established routine, Margot Miller, another guide who has since left the Abbey's employ, was directed to lock the rooms on the first floor of the South East Wing, a task she had undertaken on previous occasions without incident. A circular path took her to a small parlour directly opposite the top of the stairs, some twenty feet away. Via an adjacent dressing room, Margot went through a side door into Mrs. Webb's former bedroom from where she could make her way back using the landing door. After closing the drapes in each room she locked each door behind her totally unaware of what would confront her.

Having closed one set of drapes in the final bedroom, she passed from one window to the next, glancing into the high, baroque mirror on the wall between the two, momentarily shocked to see a 'human' shape blocking her exit. Thinking it was a companion, she calmly turned only to find the doorway filled with the ethereal form of a Cavalier, dressed in full apparel, wearing thigh boots, sword and the inevitable flamboyant feather in his hat.

Still shocked, a singular awful truth immediately filled Margot's mind; she had locked all the doors behind her and unwittingly sealed off any avenue of escape. Fearful seconds dragged as she glanced about seeking a course of action before accepting her position as futile.

Fear finally gave way to panic, screaming, she lunged towards the apparition, and passed straight through it onto the landing. In terrified flight from an imagined pursuer, Margot glanced back from the stairs, only to find herself alone. The figure had vanished!

Still appalled by this encounter, she came downstairs to bump into a workmate with whom she shared the incident. Later, having regained both composure and sense of humour, Margot laughingly added, "This was no *Laughing* Cavalier!"

A WINDOW TO ANOTHER WORLD?

Laughter without humour.

"So cold it chills me to the marrow." Byron huddles in his chair, the great black jaws of an empty fireplace mocking. "Warmth, I crave warmth, a warm body, a warm, soft, resuscitating form in which to wrap myself. He thinks of Lucy again.

"Is it my fault I attract them all, except those who really matter?"

His foot pains him, and he curses his disability, made more apparent in his melancholy, his over-indulgence. He looks down at himself and sees *' a blighted trunk upon a cursed root.'*

"Nanny," he whispers, "Nanny Smith. You knew it to be only company I craved at first. What was it you said about me after my death to that renowned gentleman Washington Irving? Ah yes, *'Poor soul!'* You said, *'He was so lame, he could not go out much with the men, all the comfort he had was to be little with the lasses.'*

"Aye and you were right, dear housekeeper, better company than the skulls, the only recompense for my own damnable search for wealth beneath the Cloisters' flags."

His laugh is as cold as the stone coffin wherein lay skulls and bones unearthed in this second frantic search for treasure!

A grunt of disdain. Black humour surfaces. "I really unnerved you all when I had that coffin placed at the entrance to the Great Hall. Ha!" He slaps the table. "Which of you would venture by it after dark? Even into my study under the stare of those two wretched skulls reposing either side of the antique cross?"

Nanny Smith reminds: *'I used to have to go into the room at night to shut the windows, and if I glanced an eye at them they all seemed to grin, which, I believe, skulls always do. I can't say but I was glad to get out of the room.'*

Byron sneers. "I dealt with it all; I continue thus. Fearsome shades compel my actions, and those of my friends...and wicked ancestor! Remember Verse 22 of 'Elegy to Newstead'?

'Graves, long with rank and sighing weeds o'erspread,
Ransack'd resign, perforce, their mortal mould:
From ruffian fangs, escape not e'en the dead,
Racked from repose, in search for buried gold'. "

He attempts to rise, his corrupted limb failing to answer and he curses. Slumping back in the chair, he remembers the tortures endured in his and his mother's efforts to seek a cure for his limitations.

"Could we return to those early years when childhood fancies took precedence over a disability. Even back before the taunts; the heartache; the disillusion.

"Newstead, great house, you and I have so much in common, that fractured allure."

IV

In those early weeks his feelings were deep seated, and prompted lines contained in his famous poem Don Juan (Canto XIII):

*'An old, old monastery once, and now
Still older mansion, of a rich and rare
Mix'd Gothic........'*

*'Huge halls, long galleries, spacious chambers, join'd
By no quite lawful marriage of the arts,
Might shock a connoisseur; but, when combined,
Form'd a whole which, irregular in parts,
Yet left a grand impression on the mind,
At least of those whose eyes are in their hearts:'*

Sadly, the young Byron would spend little time at Newstead, the house being dilapidated and barely habitable. It was almost devoid of furniture, linen or crockery, and with Catherine Byron obliged to sell their meagre possessions to pay for the journey south, and the estate so decrepit, this meant they were unable to pay for even necessary repairs or replacements.

To ease this situation, the Abbey was rented during the young Lord's minority to wealthy bachelor, Lord Grey de Ruthyn, the lease to run for over five years from Christmas, 1802.

Byron did visit Newstead periodically, but certain events were soon to have a profound effect on him and his future. He was growing up, and amongst the attractions for the fifteen-year old Byron, was Mary Chaworth 'the bright morning star' of neighbouring Annesley Hall, and two years his senior.

Diadem Hill is part of the Annesley estate. Here they would meet and finally part. After this, Annesley would lose its enchantment for the poet:

'Hills of Annesley, bleak and barren,
Where my thoughtless childhood strayed,
How the northern tempests warring,
Howl above thy tufted shade.
Now no more, the hours beguiling,
Former favourite haunts I see,
Now no more my Mary smiling,
Makes ye seem a heaven to me.'

A smitten Byron's dream of marrying Mary and ending the family feud, flowing from the celebrated duel, foundered when she said: "I could never love 'that lame boy'."

This affliction plagued him from birth. Concerning it, he wrote: *'My poor mother and after her my school fellows, by their taunts, led me to consider my lameness as the greatest misfortune, and I have never been able to conquer this feeling'.*

First sent to a charlatan in Nottingham named Lavender to be tortured without benefit, Byron was later, in 1799, sent to London by his mother to be placed under the care of Dr Matthew Baillie and Dr Laurie, who treated him for three years with better results and less pain.

Such events confused Byron's adolescent years, yet despite this his limb defect was not particularly serious. Louisa Wildman, wife of Colonel Thomas Wildman who subsequently purchased the Abbey from Byron, obtained a letter from Byron's bootmaker, one William Swift of Southwell, stating that the so-called 'club foot' problem was non-existent. He states: *'...that both his feet were equally well formed, one, however, being an inch and a half shorter than the other. The defect was not in the foot but in the ankle, which, being weak, caused the foot to turn out too much.'*

Romance and fractured allure seemed to walk hand in hand, not least furthered by the tempestuous Catherine Byron.

But then, ruinous perfection itself can remain the attraction...

CHAPTER THREE

MOTHER LOVE (?)

--oOo--

I

Overgrown, unkempt, the gardens ripple in the early breeze, a chill off the lake causes Lord Byron to shiver.

Night-time terrors disappear, no longer imbibing past memory, but restless thoughts and insecurity still torment. "From where does my gloomy temperament emerge?" He demands.

He reaches towards a new rosebud on the bush, strangled by coarse grass. He utters but one word: "Mother."

His thoughts whisper: "Aye, and even you suffered your own torment. I well recall what I said about you."

'...as haughty as Lucifer with her descent from the Stuarts and her right line from the old Gordons...always telling me how superior her Gordons were to the southern Byrons...'

He fixes on the virgin rose.

"You had a fierce temper, Catherine Gordon. You would spoil, then abuse me, hurl hot pokers and tongs at times, and cut me to the bone.

"Whilst bathing with Lord Sligo in the Mediterranean, your comments on my imperfections came to mind. *'My mother,'* I told him, *'in one of her fits of passion, uttered an imprecation upon me, praying that I might prove as ill-formed in mind as I am in body.'"*

He pauses, contemplating. "Is it those tortured forms, those graven thunder-scars which now surround me and rise up compelling me to question my own destiny...whether it be alive or dead?"

The thought subsides, and he thinks again about his mother.

"Conversely, you could be attentive and affectionate, which, God help me, I returned. Surely you know this from the number and content of the many letters I wrote you during my absences. Had I been less attentive, uncaring if you will, I would hardly have bothered. After your passing, I wrote: *'With a very large portion of foibles and irritability, she was without a vice.'*

"And you had cause to be bitter. Not over me, well not overmuch."

Catherine Gordon was the *13th* and last laird of Gight in Aberdeenshire, whose ruined castle still remains as a memorial to the wild and dissolute Clan Gordon, known as the *Gey* (reckless) Gordons, who laid claim to a terrible, treacherous and blood-filled past.

It is impossible to define the poet's character, or the influence his stewardship had on Newstead without first considering this dark background. His accession to the title linked a bloodthirsty inheritance steeped in Celtic myth and sorcery with one already renowned for its turbulence and eccentricities.

From 1560, the Clan's history is one of murder, imprisonment, suicide, execution and sudden death. Small wonder then that the spirits of those pathetic victims frequent Gight's ruins, one of them allegedly Byron's mother.

Legends, as deep and unfathomable as the mists that envelop it, cling to Gight. The 6th Laird was a wild, violent man who confessed to his wife: *'I can tak no rest. I knaw I will die up on a scaffold. Thair is ane evil turn in my hand.'* He almost lived to see his prophesy come true, dying instead in custody in Edinburgh Tolbooth.

In 1644, during the Covenanter's Revolt, the 7th Laird, who was said to practise witchcraft - knowing he would be taken prisoner and the castle looted - flung his treasure into a dark, bottomless and loathsome whirlpool in the River Ythan below the castle, known as *Hagberry Pot*. On his release from custody in 1647 he sent down a diver to recover it. After many minutes the diver surfaced terrified and bleeding, swearing that in the depths he had confronted the Devil surrounded by other monstrous creatures, using the Laird's plate and other treasure from which to eat a diabolical meal! Understandably, the poor soul refused to re-enter the water. The Laird, however, suspected that the diver planned to return later to retrieve the treasure for himself, so he ordered this pathetic man to be escorted to the castle and tortured until the hapless victim cried bitterly: *'Better face the Devil again than the Laird of Gight.'*

Back at Hagberry Pot, as the unwilling diver sank beneath the surface a second time, the water seethed, and moments later the sight of his quartered body with a knife driven into his still quivering heart, sent all the onlookers on the bank insane - except of course the Laird!

The hagberry, or bird cherry, still grows about Hagberry Pot and is reputedly the main ingredient of *witches' brew.*

A hint of diabolism practised by the Laird of Gight? We may never know. Certainly a subterranean cavern - *Craig's Horror* - exists. Its labyrinthine passages disappear into uncharted darkness. One attempt to discover where they led resulted in a piper being sent into them. As the shadows swallowed him, the sound of pipes gradually faded until it finally ceased. The piper never returned, but on the darkest of nights Craig's Horror echoes with their mournful dirge.

Byron looks across the lake, the rose forgotten; the chill of morning given over to a deeper chill in his soul. Oh the horrors of his forebears; what foulness inflicted.

"I am plagued by the relevance of the number 13 concerning myself, and my mother."

In 1785, whilst visiting Bath, Catherine met the dissipated Captain John Byron, known as 'Mad Jack'. This immoral eldest son of 'Foulweather Jack', was a widower seeking an heiress to finance his life of drinking and gambling. He was already notorious from his celebrated affair with Amelia, Lady Carmarthen, whom he subsequently married after her divorce on the grounds of their adultery. A number of children were born, the youngest being Augusta, Byron's half sister with whom the 6th Lord would fall hopelessly in love. Lady

Carmarthen died in 1784 leaving her handsome husband penniless.

'Mad Jack' then enticed Catherine Gordon into his net. She fell for him and remained infatuated with him for the rest of his life, despite his intemperance. They soon married, though he openly admitted that he had only married her for money. All but Catherine seemed able to see the outcome of the match. The following verse appeared in Peter Buchan's 'Collection of Bards', published at the time:

> *'O where are ye goein', bonny Miss Gordon,*
> *O where are ye goein' sae bonnie and braw,*
> *Ye've married ye've married wi' Johnny Byron,*
> *To squander the lands of Gight awa'.*

> *'This youth is a rake, frae England he's come,*
> *The Scots dinna ken his extraction ava;*
> *He keeps up his misses, his landlord he duns;*
> *That's fast drawin' the lands o' Gight awa'.*

Amongst other assets, Catherine brought with her estates in Gight and Manskill, Aberdeenshire; two salmon fisheries on the River Dee, and shares in the Aberdeen Banking Company. Soon she was reduced to living on an income of £150 a year. As 'Mad Jack' gambled and drank his way through her fortune, Gight had to be sold, but not before it had been stripped of saleable timber.

A strange and intriguing inheritance of the 6th Lord from both his parents is a future peculiarly susceptible to prophesy. The ancient sage, Thomas the Rhymer, wrote:

'When the herons leave the tree
The laird o' Gight shall landless be'.

As woods were cleared for timber, nesting herons were disturbed. The birds flew to the adjoining estate of Lord Haddo, another branch of Clan Gordon.

Lord Haddo eventually bought Gight and installed his twenty seven year old son, another George Gordon, and his family. Gight would exact its revenge for these insults, and once again Thomas the Rhymer predicted:

'At Gight three men a violent death shall dee,
And after that the lands shall lie in lea'.

George Gordon met his death on the 2nd October 1791 in a riding accident in the castle grounds. His ghost can still be seen riding through the avenue of trees before the ruin. Shortly after this two servants met a violent end, and thus secured the cursed place's abandonment.

There are so many comparisons here with Devil Byron, whose shade gallops through Newstead's grounds; who allegedly practised witchcraft; who dragged the ponds at Newstead for treasure, and who, it could be said, eventually lost his senses.

'Mad Jack' and Catherine fled to France to avoid creditors, but Catherine returned to England for the birth of their son whom she brought to live in Aberdeen. Her dissolute husband remained in France where he died on the 2nd August 1791.

It is hardly surprising that this proud woman should feel at odds with a world that had treated her thus, and whose son would appear to have inherited the violence and virtues of both sides of the family.

Above all, she remained his *'...one friend in the world...'* and one of the four most prominent women in his short life.

He lingers on the shore of the lake, with only wild bird-cries for company.

"Yes, Catherine, Mother, my one friend in the world. Yet we could not live with each other. You drove me from England, you and Mary."

At twenty-one, and still troubled by debt, Byron borrowed £4800 from Scrope Davies to finance an extended tour through Mediterranean countries. Whilst there, he would pass through the Greek town of Missolonghi where, fifteen years later, he would die.

On the eve of his departure for Greece, Byron's thoughts returned to Mary Chaworth, a wound not yet healed. Prompted again by this sorry chapter, he wrote:

'And I will cross the whitening foam...seek a foreign home...Till I forget a fair, false face...But ever love, and love but one.'

The melancholy accompanying Byron's departure from England returned as he again set eyes on its shores. At sea he had written from the frigate *Volgate* to Francis Hodgson: *'I am returning home without a hope, and almost without a desire... In short I am sick and sorry, and when I have a little repaired my irreparable affairs away I shall march.'*

During his tour, Byron would still carry fond memories of England, and especially Nottinghamshire. Still beset by financial problems, he wrote to his lawer John Hanson: *'It is in the power of* God, the Devil and Man, *to make me poor and miserable, but neither the* second *nor* third *shall make me sell Newstead.'*

During Byron's absence, Catherine had installed herself at the Abbey, whose ruined, draught-ridden halls and rooms, coupled with constant worry over her son and money, and a predilection to liquor, conspired to herald her weakening, and subsequent demise.

Over-riding this was the presentiment formed from her claimed Celtic gift for second sight that she would never see her son again.

She seemed particularly troubled by the execution of a debt for £1600, suddenly levied by a Mr. Brothers of Nottingham, an upholsterer. On the verge of bankruptcy, Brothers was desperate, and Catherine feared that her son would be blamed for the destitution of Brothers and his family. She suffered a massive heart attack.

As she lay dying, her words to her maid were: *'If I should be dead when Byron comes down what a strange thing it would be.'*

She died on the 1st August 1811, at the early age of forty-six, old beyond her years through a life of constant financial chaos, yet still absolutely devoted to one, single human being - her beloved son. At this time, he was still not aware of his mother's condition, which is perhaps fortunate.

To compound this melancholy, and so soon after his mother's funeral, Byron learnt of the death of Charles Skinner Mathews, drowned at Cambridge in the River

Cam, together with the death of three other friends from his days at Harrow and Cambridge - perhaps a further echo of Thomas the Rhymer's prediction concerning the Gight connection. This loss forced Byron into demanding Scrope Davies join him at Newstead admitting to him that, *'Some curse hangs over me and mine.'*

Legacy again? Or perhaps a grim reminder of Mother Shipton's curse.

Significantly, when we examine the Gordon family's traits very often leaning towards melancholy and suicide, we find it easier to understand Byron's own inclinations which led him to write to publisher John Murray: *'I had always been told that in temper I more resembled my maternal Grandfather than any of my father's family...that is the gloomier part of his temper...'*

Did his ancestors call from the past, demanding he join them?

A propensity to colour each event in pessimistic hue, and to uphold an unshakable belief in omens may have conferred upon him a distorted view of life. His great-grandfather, Alexander Gordon, the 11th Laird, had drowned himself in the River Ythan in January 1760. Nineteen years later to the month, when Catherine was only fifteen years old, his grandfather, George Gordon, the 12th Laird and after whom Byron was named, similarly ended his life in the Canal at Bath. It would be no surprise if Byron considered following their example.

Byron shakes his head, the past affecting him far more than he will admit.

"Desperate times," he muses quietly. "They always return to *haunt* me."

Lingering by the roses once more, he muses that perhaps the scent of last year's full-blown blooms attaches itself to him *and* the gaunt building behind...

Unthinking, he glances up at implacable windows. "Have you really gone, sweet Catherine? Really left me?"

He detects a shape at the Library window...

II

A round, bespectacled face peers back, looks straight at him, a puzzled frown on it there and gone. "Did I see something in the garden just now?" Pauline Corby speaks aloud to no-one in particular. "It's probably a visitor." She shrugs, turns back to the two men interviewing her and says: "I quite love this room. It is where I first smelled the roses on the table. I was doing this business, moving curtains and the like, I even went to the other side and did the same, but it was here."

Pauline Corby is a quiet, sober, dignified lady, who commenced working at the Abbey in 1988. Lifting her hand from one of the two oak tables inlaid with leather, she glances around the library, or North Gallery, today known as the Byron Gallery as if expecting a visitor.

A long, narrow, room with a door at either end, its walls are lined with bookshelves and glass cases housing some of the Abbey's collection of Byronic memorabilia. Heavy drapes and blinds - barriers against damaging sunlight on priceless furniture and artefacts - frame 19th Century oriel windows situated either side of the

47

fireplace, the windows overlooking what was once the nave of the old Church. The outlook across the grass towards the haunted grove reflects the peace within, and it becomes easy to realise why, in this room more than any other at Newstead, one becomes less aware of time quietly slipping by.

On a cold, bright morning in early April 1990, sunshine elongates the shadows across garden and lake. Outside, the first of the spring flowers, daffodils, crocuses and a few brave tulips hint at the profusion to come.

"I was polishing this table" - Pauline indicates one of the large, rectangular and heavy tables - "when I became aware of the most beautiful smell, an old fashioned smell. I looked round, convinced someone had walked in with a bunch of flowers, or was perhaps wearing perfume - but no - and I knew it couldn't be polish, as we only use odourless beeswax polish here."

She stroked the tabletop lightly. "I thought maybe someone had left potpourri nearby, so I checked everywhere, behind drapes, in corners, beneath furniture - nothing. Then I noticed the strangest thing - every time I moved away from the table the smell gradually dissipated. Only when I moved back again was it as strong as ever, and centred around the table."

Again she glances at the table. "I felt something funny was happening, but I didn't feel afraid. I simply carried on. You see, I didn't believe in ghosts or anything then. I'm still what you'd call a 'sceptic', but certain things have occurred here that I can't explain."

From this time, whenever she walked through the Nursery attics, Pauline would often detect that same perfume, a delicate scent that reminded her of wild roses. And for some inexplicable reason, she became convinced that this scent belonged to a woman - a person rather than an object.

"Whenever I detected it I would say aloud: *'Oh, you're here again.'* It didn't worry me because whatever it was didn't appear threatening. In fact I didn't think any more about it, just accepted it until that plane incident. *That shook me, it really shook me!"*

In March 1995, Pauline went on vacation with a friend to the USA and visited San Francisco on the west coast. The return flight to Heathrow is a journey she will never forget.

One of the disadvantages of flying long-haul can be boredom.

In a sense in-flight passengers are incarcerated for the flight's duration. As a child will seek alternatives to play, so adults seek various avenues of escaping monotony. In so doing we tend to lower our defences and sometimes allow invasion of our private thoughts by others, often entering into conversation with complete strangers beside whom we have been placed arbitrarily.

Pauline was no exception. Having perhaps exhausted conversation with her friend, maybe read a little, enjoyed a meal, taken advantage of in-flight entertainment, she felt drawn towards a different outlet.

Amidst the bustle of cabin staff and passengers, Pauline found herself making small talk with her neighbour across the aisle. This person, a lady from

Carmel, California, explained she was travelling to England on business. She was a writer who *'received spirit messages from dead poets'*. "I then write about them," she added.

Interest enlivened, and reminded of her own experiences at Newstead Abbey, Pauline asked: "Do you *hear* anything from Lord Byron?"

"No, I don't. Wordsworth, Shelley, Robert Burns, but not Byron. In fact I know very little about him."

Pauline then enthusiastically proceeded to enlighten her adding, "He lived at Newstead Abbey in Nottinghamshire."

Noting her fellow passenger's puzzlement, Pauline added jokingly: "Robin Hood country?"

Recognising this familiar legendary name, the American said jokingly, "Ah, Kevin Costner."

Pauline smiled at her co-passenger's obvious limited knowledge.

"Where is Newstead situated in relation to London?" ventured the lady. "I might visit."

Flippantly, Pauline answered, "Oh, from the map it's straight up and left a bit".

A drinks trolley and a smiling stewardess interrupted them, the two retiring to their own thoughts. A few minutes later Pauline felt a very light touch on her arm which she described as being,'...like that of a kitten, or puppy pawing'.

The woman had leaned across and looking intensely at Pauline said: "Now tell me about the roses."

Overawed, and perhaps a little shocked by the revelation, Pauline was forced to consider their earlier conversation. "I was speechless," she said, "I'd only just met this person, so how on earth could she have any conception of my experiences years ago? Nothing whatever had been mentioned about roses.

"Instinctively, and without knowing why, I said: 'It's a woman. Will I ever see her?'"

Again, eyes met, registering to Pauline's mounting disquiet that there were to be further disclosures.

Meaningfully, the lady replied: "I do not know if it will be *given* to you."

Intrusive sounds dulled, self-imposed isolation forgotten, both seemingly suspended in space and time, as though kindred spirits had met. *But*, more than that, it was as though another indefinable element had joined them.

Pauline mulled this over, rightly or wrongly assuming she may be granted the gift of sight, which suggested *sight of the spirit,* or presence.

The author, elaborating on this, told her, "Next time you smell the scent of roses, close your eyes and you may *feel* or *hear* the swish of her clothes."

With that the conversation ended, as both tried to reconcile what had passed between them. Might there be an explanation?

The lady had revealed that she 'talked' with dead poets, but knew little of Byron and even less of Newstead. Had she read Pauline's mind? If true, a remarkable feat in itself.

Had Pauline carried this scent with her from Newstead? Was she an unwitting link by which whatever power thrives at Newstead had reached out to touch another, possibly sympathetic agent - the American author? It is a forbidding thought, and one not easily dismissed.

Back at the Abbey had Pauline heard or even seen the wearer of that perfume yet?

"No, but I still occasionally smell the roses."

Is there any pattern to it?

"Not really, the smell of roses can come anytime. Sometimes you get two incidents close together."

Could the reason be evident within Byron's lines to his mother: '*I have brought you a shawl, and a quantity of Attar of Roses, but these I must smuggle if possible.*'

So, might Catherine Gordon Byron, whose own ancestors practised witchcraft and sorcery, rather than linger in the sad, deserted ruin of Gight Castle, her ancestral home, tarry at Newstead, close to her precious, only child buried a short distance away?

Whilst open to conjecture, we do know that Pauline Corby's plane incident 'really *shook* her.' And that this, and other occurrences, have opened her eyes to a different world and its varied possibilities, for she is not the only one to be aware of the smell of roses at the Abbey.

III

For a smell to impregnate a house and remain can often be explained - the odour of paint will linger for ages after decorating has been completed, the aroma of a particularly fine cigar long after the smoker has departed a room.

What then is that sweet, sickly fragrance which clings to the Dressing Room adjoining the Charles II

Room, and often commented upon by visitors to the house?

A clue lies in the title of the room itself, wherein guests would repair to their toilet. In the 17th and 18th Centuries wigs were fashionable and wig powder was used liberally to hide the join between it and the owner's real hair, some of the powder inevitably finding its way between floorboards, its redolence attached to the room's very fabric.

This room is not entirely innocent inasmuch as visitors to the Abbey have often been heard to comment: "I didn't like it up there, I didn't like that room."

The unfamiliar aroma could prompt this reaction. As one guide says: "I don't know what wig powder smells like, but if you detect something that is totally foreign..." The statement is left hanging, prompting unease, and will emphasise the experiences of certain staff members.

Such odours cling to specific rooms, and can generally be detected. But if certain odours move to different parts of the house, have they then become attached to a person rather than a place, and thus create their own intriguing scent?

The landing immediately outside the South Drawing Room, the room used by Catherine Gordon Byron, is where the smell of roses is most prevalent, visitors often retracing their steps to re-acquaint themselves with it.

Guide Susan Patching is smart in appearance, her dark suit and short, fair hair striking an academic note. Certainly she loves books, especially those concerning the Byron family about whom she has read widely.

Recollecting one particular incident, Sue relates that whilst on duty at the top of the stairs in the South East

Wing, a woman visitor returned more than once to that landing. "I just couldn't understand what she was up to. I thought: what is she doing? Then she came down and said: 'I bet you wondered what's been the matter with me. I've been trying to trace this smell of roses.'

"I asked her where the smell came from and she answered: 'It's the closed door up there. It's coming from there, and it's very strong.'"

Often familiar fragrances herald the arrival of their owners, or offer clues to their, as yet, unnoticed proximity. Yet, if their wearer remains unseen, a perfume, or scent, alone betraying their presence, this may pre-empt a very different assumption, in this case, that Catherine Gordon Byron is once more in residence.

Maisie Hammond, a bubbly, diminutive lady with a marvellous sense of humour commenced in her position as Housekeeper at the Abbey on the 21st May 1984. To date, a good track record notwithstanding she held doubts about being offered the post.

Even at the onset, Maisie felt she *belonged* here. Certainly human intervention and discussion made the decision, for three weeks after the interview she received a telephone call to ask: "Would you like the position?" But, we may wonder who else felt she belonged there! The rest, as they say, is history.

Heavy drapes filter diffuse light through small leaded windows onto the shallow, red carpeted, dark oak stairs beyond the shadowed entrance hall. The stairs lead to a first floor landing in the west wing from whose walls portraits of the rather austere Victorian family, Webb, peer stonily down. To the right, a table and chairs wait as a place of respite, or quiet contemplation. The soft, regular tock of the grandfather clock is a heartbeat in the silence.

Prior to the commencement of her first main season at the Abbey, Maisie attends to her chores. She is quite alone.

Behind her, closed doors leading to untenanted rooms that will later require her deft, caring touch, remain impassive.

"My first experience was smelling roses," she explains. "I was in the entrance hall, and then moved to this first floor landing by the radiator. It was such a strong smell that I chased after Jane, another guide, and asked: 'Jane, have you just sprayed yourself with perfume?'"

A bemused Jane replied: "No, I don't use perfume."

Maisie sniffed the air. "There's a very strange smell in here." But Maisie promptly dismissed it as being just another smell in the house, until -

"...We hired another volunteer lady. I was cleaning and wiping a table on the first floor landing, when Angela came down the stairs that lead to the nursery. Putting her head over the banister she said, 'Oh Maisie, what a lovely perfumed polish, what is it?'"

A conscientious woman, Maisie expects others to share her standards, but is, at the same time, always prepared to pass on her knowledge to those less experienced. She lightly admonished her companion, "Angela, you're not allowed to use perfumed polish here.

This is wax, pure beeswax. That's all you're allowed to use."

Maisie went on to detail the methods adopted to preserve the furniture.

Angela, grateful for the tip, turned to go about her business; then quickly held up her hand to silence Maisie. Astonished, Angela said, "The smell, it's just wafted under my nose going back up these stairs. It's like a big bouquet of roses, beautiful perfumed roses."

"But it's April," pointed out a bewildered Maisie, "there isn't a rose anywhere near the place, neither inside, or growing in the gardens."

They lapsed into silence, neither wishing to voice the obvious question. But after this, Maisie no longer dismissed the scent as *just another smell in the house.*

The next time she saw Angela, Maisie asked her to write down the date she came to Newstead. "Just to see if it holds any significance because *it was at the beginning of my first season when I smelt the roses.*"

Maisie smiles. "You see, for someone else to come here and say this, then I think to myself...I'm not so daft after all."

And how does Maisie describe the scent?

"It's an old-fashioned rose smell, not one you associate with modern perfumes, more a musky sort of smell. Not strong. It puts a nice scent into the air.

"At times, when I'm walking elsewhere in the house, say along a passageway, I think: Ah, I can smell wood burning. If you think of being inside a building like Newstead, it kind of takes you back quite a way because you then think to yourself: old newspapers wrapped around fresh kindling sticks. You can smell that..."

And the aroma of wood smoke is evidence of a supernatural presence.

CHAPTER FOUR

INDULGENCES

--oOo--

I

The mist shrouding the lake gradually clears, a watery sun winks through parting clouds, and Byron contemplates nature, his literary mind forever composing.

"I awoke one morning and found myself famous." His chuckle is humorous, and at the same time holds a touch of irony. "But I ask, what did fame bring me?

"Darkness and ghosts ceased to plague me after *Childe Harold's Pilgrimage* was published at the end of February 1812. Bless me, only a few days later I took my seat in the House of Lords.

"Women flocked to my door: I became the toast of London. I was the fashion. Absurd but I couldn't help it. Naturally my affairs were talked about, but then women, damn me all those women! Especially stupid, fey Lady Caroline. None of 'em brought in any money, rather they spent it, and how could I, a gentleman, accept payment for my work? Lifestyle cost me dearly in later years.

"In March 1809, I did write Mother words to the effect that Newstead *and I* stand *or fall together. I have now lived on the spot, I have fixed my heart upon it, no pressure, present or future, shall induce me to barter the last vestige of our inheritance...but could I obtain for Newstead Abbey the finest fortune in the country I would reject the proposition...*

"Then wouldn't you know, three years later Newstead was up for sale by auction with mixed results. It never reached the reserve I placed on it and I was forced to withdraw it. Shortly afterwards, a gentleman named Claughton agreed to buy it by private treaty for £140,000. He only ever managed to raise £28,000 and the sale fell through. I did manage to retain £25,000 of Claughton's money, which went some way to alleviating my problems. Certainly it was on the cards that Newstead would unfortunately need to be sold, but I waived the option for the present time."

Over-indulgence jades the appetite, pursuits become boring, indeed tiring and we wonder if Byron's frenetic, fanatical carousing was a desperate attempt to compensate for perceived inadequacies and the consequences of misplaced affection. Whatever the reason it could never be sufficient to overcome the depths to which a man sinks before he either drowns in deprivation, or seeks salvation.

In 1815, once more tiring of a dissolute lifestyle, Byron decided upon a different form of escape.

"I had periodically toyed with the idea of marriage, perhaps selfishly seeing it as a partial solution to my financial problems. Less than a month after my mother's death I recall writing to Augusta: *'If I can't persuade some wealthy dowdy to ennoble the dirty puddle of her mercantile blood - why - I shall leave England and all its clouds for the east again; I am very sick of it already.'* In hindsight, I admit that this is a very revealing passage in terms of my personality, prejudices and financial straits at that time."

Reflections still in the lake, his contemplation, his admissions forcing him to admit even more of his somewhat deprived upbringing.

"I know that I had not been taught in the ways of the English aristocracy because my impoverished childhood had been spent many miles from my inheritance, and far from the trappings and lifestyle granted to the son of a noble family."

He shakes his head, a grin hardly humorous. "Lacking a role model I could only mimic and adopt what I perceived as being the manners of a nobleman."

Byron paces like some irate thespian: he punches the air, emphasising his own admissions. "So what if I was egotistical, and damned proud? I often spoke of *'...men of my own rank.'* Even on the day I inherited the title, I asked Mother if she could see any difference in me since I became a lord. After all, was I not marked as being special?"

As Lady Blessington observed when she visited him in Italy in 1822: *'I never met anyone with so decided a taste for aristocracy as Lord Byron...Were he sensible how much the Lord is overlooked in the* Poet *he would be less vain of his rank; but as it is, this vanity is very prominent, and resembles more the pride of a parvenue than the calm dignity of an ancient aristocrat.'*

He stands beneath the Gothic arch of the West Front, and inspects the eroded stone, legacy of centuries of erosion and misuse. Blank, pitted faces return his stare.

"Blast you, ancient church. Was it you gave me blessing to marry?" A fist beats the stone. "But is it not true that a man needs a wife of his own, and not always the use of someone else's partner?"

Annabella Milbanke, a quiet, self-possessed and intellectual girl had attracted numerous suitors before meeting Lord Byron. She was four years his junior, and the only child of Sir Ralph Milbanke of Seaham, County Durham. Lady Elizabeth Foster (later Duchess of Devonshire) said of her: *'She is good, amiable and sensible, but cold, prudent and reflecting... She is really an icicle.'*

The couple's first meeting at Melbourne House, Whitehall, initiated her long diary entries, which chronicled their growing friendship. She wrote of Byron: *'that he is sincerely repentant for the evil he has done, though he has not resolution (without aid) to adopt a new course of conduct and feelings'.*

As their relationship developed the poet wrote in his Journal: *'What an odd situation and friendship is ours! - without one spark of love on either side...She is a poetess - a mathematician - a metaphysician, and yet, withal, very kind, generous, and gentle, with very little pretension'.*

Years later Byron commented to Thomas Medwin a cousin of the poet, Shelley *'There was something piquant, and what we term pretty, in Miss Milbanke...figure perfect for her height.'*

Despite his misgivings, *'she is a little encumbered with virtue,'* he proposed in 1812 and was duly rejected. Her reasons, to her, were perfectly logical - he did not measure up to the exacting standards she expected of a future partner. It is worth noting that 'she expected her husband's feelings to be commanded by reason and would not marry into a family in which there was a tendency to insanity'.

Years earlier, observing the activities of the young Byron and his cronies at Newstead, and hardly able to forget the 5th Lord, the locals became convinced that insanity was an inherent feature of the Byron family.

"A mistake, my one, true friend," he says aloud as he relaxes on the steps of Boatswain's tomb. "I should have left it there, but when Annabella re-opened our correspondence after all those months I was flattered into making a second proposal - promptly accepted.

"But I was always my own man and would neither bend nor change for anyone. Annabella mistakenly believed she could reform me. At first it amused me to learn how easily shocked she became, but I soon grew alarmed at her ability to draw inferences from any careless word or amusing taunt. She forgets she had married a man of words!

Two irreconcilable personalities - myself the determined lord and she my 'Princess of Parallelograms', coined following my remark: *'Sometimes we are too alike, and then again too unlike. This comes of system, and squaring of her notions to the devil knows what'.*"

The seeds of the future were sown when they married on 2nd January, 1815.

The marriage appeared doomed from the outset. On the eve of the wedding, Byron's thoughts returned to Mary Chaworth. Later, at the Villa Diodati, he would pen 'The Dream':

> '...*before an altar - with a gentle bride:*
> *Her face was fair, but was not that which made*
> *The starlight of his boyhood; - as he stood*
> *Even at the altar, o'er his brow there came*
> *The self same aspect, and the quivering shock*
> *That in the antique oratory shook*
> *His bosom in its solitude...*'

Nonetheless, the marriage was sanctified. They lived in London, and their daughter Augusta Ada was born on the 10th December that same year. They never lived at Newstead, Byron's financial circumstances making it imperative he sell it as soon as possible. He told Frances Hodgson with whom he was at Cambridge that if Annabella ever went there she was certain to become attached to it and thus thwart his plans.

II

Byron stirs, relaxing on the bed. He opens his palm to reveal and to contemplate a miniature.

"Aye, a veritable vixen had infiltrated my lair, so convinced of her infallibility. What a clever, calculating and manipulative woman you turned out to be. Was I wrong to insist you should bear no blame for the breakdown of our marriage?"

This naive act of chivalry, capitalised on by a woman with few scruples and quite capable of using deceit and her own imagined ill-health to gain sympathy, would cost Byron dear. She relied upon a coterie of subservient admirers to spread her insinuations without her ever going into specifics regarding her husband's conduct.

On the 13th February, 1816, soon after they had separated on the 15th January, Annabella wrote the following to Byron: *'It can be fully and clearly proved that I left your house under the persuasion of your having a complaint of so dangerous a nature that my agitation might bring on a fatal crisis... I have consistently fulfilled my duty as your wife. It was too dear to be resigned til it became hopeless. Now my resolution cannot be changed.'*

She later wrote: *'Previously to my departure, it had been strongly impressed on my mind, that Lord Byron was under the influence of* insanity.'

Ensuing accounts from others in respect of life with Byron illustrate how irritable and unpredictable he could be. The poet could descend into *'...wild and hysterical storms of fury...his white and even teeth would flash and clash as those of a panther; when he would scream aloud in his vexation...'* Composed, controlled, Annabella would have no experience of anything like this nor any idea of how she might handle it.

He places the miniature face down on the bed. "But is not anger merely another face of passion? And did you fear that passion might melt your protective shield of ice?"

A small, square-standing mirror throws back his reflection, his haughty autocratic bearing perhaps dulled somewhat, yet still apparent. He shrugs, still reflecting on Annabella. "Ah, dear heart, what else may one be but chivalrous? For chivalry is a part of every gentleman's nature no matter what it costs."

Eyes in the mirror, and on the past. "I feel that history should be the judge, the public my jurors on the truths contained in my memoirs."

Byron is wrong.

Ironically, his own version of events was lost when those memoirs, containing a full account of the marriage, were burned by Annabella's representative, Colonel Doyle, in the fire grate at publisher John Murray's. It was done with the connivance of Byron's successor, the 7th Lord, shortly after the poet's death and left Annabella's own version of events publicly unchallenged, Byron's earlier behaviour sufficient to condemn him.

Four years earlier, in 1812, and perhaps throwing caution to the wind, an outspoken Lord Byron outraged the Establishment by speaking out against measures proposed by the Government.

In his maiden speech in the House of Lords, he condemned proposals to impose the death penalty on the Luddites, and tried to have the Bill amended.

"I had witnessed the effects of poverty all around Newstead. Indeed, I prophesied the results of the Government's failure to address Irish wrongs and entered my plea for Catholic emancipation..."

An issue over which lives are still being lost today.

It is also apparent that this Lord Byron, in a gesture reminiscent of his Cavalier ancestors, was prepared to sacrifice himself on the altar of his principles. His courage here is underlined when, in 1801, his chivalry upon seeing his friend Robert Peel being beaten by the school bully prompted a quivering Byron to offer himself for half the punishment.

Now, fearing a stout defence, his enemies chose not to wage war against Byron's beliefs, opting instead for the less retaliatory method of attacking his morals. Naturally, they put aside their own questionable behaviour, adultery being a sport practised by many.

These ferocious onslaughts and public debates prompted a preacher in Kennington, who had never met Byron, to declare: "Having drained the cup of sin to its dregs, he (Byron) is no longer human but a cool unconcerned fiend."

Earlier, in 1801, Mrs. Williams, a fortune-teller from Cheltenham, revealed to Byron's mother that the years *1816* and *1824* would be fateful ones for her son.

Could it be possible that Mrs. Williams had, herself, become attuned to Mother Shipton's earlier prophesy? Even if she had, her readings would have more profound consequences.

Combined, these effects would propel Byron to leave England for a second time, and to meet an untimely death, this time in self-imposed exile.

CHAPTER FIVE

REMINISCENCES

-oOo-

I

"JOE! Joe Murray," Byron calls, "have you attended to my brace of pistols?"

Silence settles over the Cloisters, dull echoes chased away, the quiet invaded by hurrying footsteps as the manservant hastens to wait on his master.

"'What beck'ning ghost'," Byron quotes Shakespeare softly, almost an aside, yet one with a fuller meaning as Joe enters the Great Hall by its far door.

"Your pistols, m'lord." Joe holds them out towards Byron.

Byron takes the weapons. "Ah, my protection should that damned night-time visitor pay a last visit. Think me foolish if you will, but -"

"Night-time visitor?" Joe queries.

"You're a fine one to question my motives, Joe. Do dreams and ghosts not now frighten you, though you profess never to have been superstitious for seventy-six years hitherto? But, of course," Byron smirks, "there are no ghosts."

An awkward silence prevails. Joe searches for a reply but before he can answer a light step sounds at the door, that and the swish of skirts preceding Nanny Smith's quiet knock prior to her entering the room.

Byron, alerted to her presence, grins. "Nanny, what nonsense they tell about ghosts, as if there were such things! I have never seen anything of any kind about the Abbey and I warrant you have not."

The woman remains impassive, and throws back, "Why master, you contradict yourself. I remember you telling me not many nights ago that something all black and hairy had visited you, and that you thought it was the devil."

Byron glances at the pistols, and realises that maybe his need for them is now well-founded following Nanny Smith's reminder!

Addressing Joe Murray, whose face is a bemused mask, Byron needs to know what Joe thinks, what he believes.

"I dunna like to talk o' such things, m'lord." Joe scratches his bushy side-whiskers as he contemplates. "I might add though that things ain't been right since you lifted that stone coffin from the Cloisters."

Nanny steps forward. "S'cuse me, sir, but I believe Joe is right in what he says. Beg pardon, but you know I never liked those skulls, them ones you keep in your study. And the other night something else really strange happened.

"Whilst scrubbing the floor of the little dining room after dark, at the end of the long gallery, I heard footsteps in the great hall, like the tramp of a horse. I took the light and went to see what it was. I heard them coming from the lower end of the hall to the fireplace in the centre, where they stopped: but I could see nothing. I returned to my work and in a little time heard the same noise again. I went again with the light, the footsteps stopped at the fireplace as before; still I could see nothing. When I heard the steps for the third time. I went into the hall without a light, but the steps stopped just the same, by the fireplace, halfway up the hall: when it was finished, I took the light and went through the hall, as that was my way to the kitchen. I heard no more footsteps, and thought no more of the matter, when, on coming to the lower end of the hall, I found the door locked, and then, on one side of the door, I saw the stone coffin, with the skull and bones, that had been dug up in the cloisters."

"Come, come Nanny, please be calm." Byron is clearly affected by her revelation but makes every effort to avoid its implications.

Nanny Smith meets his eyes, aware of the turmoil, which apparently seethes within his mind. Despite this, she cannot help herself, and to both Byron and Joe, states: "Mark me, both of you, there is more to come in this house, both now and in the future...The distant future, when we are no longer here...certainly not in our present form."

"What are you saying, woman?" Joe interrupts garrulously, some of this apparently lost on him. "What form then?"

Byron avoids their eyes, particularly those of Nanny Smith, and mutters as though to himself, "We have no forms, beyond the elements of which we are the mind and principle -" He smiles grimly, adding: "But choose a form - in that we will appear."

"I don't know much about that, m'lord. But do you not hear the sounds they make? It bodes ill to disturb the long dead. They wait...and watch...for always. There'll be another such as me, cleanin' and doin', and she'll see. Mark me, *she'll see!*"

II

And Nanny Smith is right...

Petite Barbara Holton left the Abbey's employ in late 1997. The longest serving member of Newstead's staff, she had worked there almost continuously for thirty years. Like all new staff members, the house vetted her. Like her colleagues, she took her duties seriously.

During those first few months of service, whilst busy in the Crypt, now the main entrance hall, she knelt before a stone tomb - bought to Newstead from Colwick Hall - in order to clean it. Hardly something you would expect a novice to be asked to undertake! Unexpectedly, she felt the weight of a hand pressed to the crown of her head as if in some divine benediction.

"I went all cold," she states. "It went right through me. I thought someone was mucking about but there was nobody there. I wasn't afraid; it was almost an uplifting experience, as though I were being blessed. Luckily it was all that happened, otherwise I might have been really scared. Weeks later I mentioned the episode to a lady who professed to be a medium and who told me: 'Maybe someone was blessing you, expressing its appreciation, and saying: 'You'll do.'"

So, what does emanate from that stone coffin? Could it be the Black Friar's new residence?

Byron warms himself by the fireplace. "Such prophetic insight does not go without consideration. But then is it true that all things of this nature should be bad? Evil? Can there not be some redeeming circumstance?"

"Aye, the master's right, woman," Joe Murray states gruffly.

Nanny whirls on Joe. "Oh you can talk, Joe Murray. Why *you* confessed to *me* you was frit by dreams and ghosts."

Although aware of her own weaknesses, Nanny is determined she will not be singled out. Turning to Byron, she says, "And you, master, have you not complained of feeling sudden chills in the midst of summer?"

Byron, far from denying this, nods agreement. "So what bearing has this on the future, Nanny? For I feel an embracing foetid chill cloaking me such as that which emanates from the lake on a winter's day."

The future handles itself...

III

Brian Ayers is, in his own way, like Byron inasmuch as he is now 'caretaker' of Newstead Abbey. Above all, he seems unconcerned by what he might confront there.

In the summer of 1987, he hadn't been at Newstead very long. "It was a scorching hot day and I was busy checking Byron's bedroom. When I'd finished, I came down into the Cloisters."

THE CUSTODIAN

The Abbey authorities employ Brian as Custodian. A calm, articulate man who has what he would describe as 'the best job in the world', is fairly tall and wiry, and capable of dealing with any problem, however insurmountable. But then the Abbey is sometimes an awkward, and often belligerent tutor.

"It never bothers me to go up there. I've never seen anything. But this particular day, as soon as I entered the Cloisters, it felt like I was stepping into a fridge. I started shivering, even my teeth chattered. I just couldn't get warm, nor understand why, because it was so hot that day."

The Cloisters are certainly cool and airy, but never freezing. At their centre is the Prior's Garden, once again a medieval herbarium. In summer doors leading to it are left permanently open.

Brian couldn't get warm for the rest of the day. "It was like having a freezing cloak cast over your shoulders. At first I thought I might be coming down with 'flu. When I reached the entrance in the main reception area, I saw our guide, Elizabeth, talking to two American women. I approached them, all three turned. I saw the look on their faces - not just surprise - something more.

"Elizabeth yelled: 'Don't come any closer', and threw out her arm as though trying to ward me off. Strangely, they all started shivering, one of the American guests saying, 'We're going, it's freezing here'. And they left."

Brian refuses to speculate on what did affect him on that day: he remains positive it was not the onset of an illness. "If it had been, then why did everyone else feel the cold when I went near them?"

Until this time Brian Ayers had been unconcerned by Newstead's reputation. He felt at ease. To him the sharp scent of old polish, the dusty aroma of ancient fabrics, the building's creaks and groans, even its dark, gloomy recesses, were hardly sinister, more like the flexing and stretching of an old friend. Yet from the moment that arctic chill settled about him, he came to realise that he had become a part of no ordinary place.

"It was the same throughout the day, shivering, teeth chattering. At one time I thought about going home - I didn't live here then, nor did I feel ill, just couldn't get warm. But I had a job to do, so I stayed until we closed.

"Mind you, it was a long day and tiring. Shivering and shaking all day didn't help. Everyone wore thin summer clothes while I needed my winter overcoat!"

In due course Brian completed his final rounds, locked up and went home.

"I thought that once I got outside I'd be all right. My car had been standing in the sun all day with its windows closed and was like a furnace inside. If anything should have thawed me out I thought that would. But I still shivered. Before I could drive off I had to get the engine warm and put the heater on full blast. Even then I couldn't get warm!

"It wasn't until I'd spent half an hour in front of my lounge gas fire with a hot cup of tea that I stopped shaking. I've never experienced anything like it, neither before nor since."

Many have experienced a sudden chill at Newstead but none in more dramatic circumstances than Brian Ayers.

"It's the Abbey's way of getting to know you," is Brian's theory. And rightly perhaps, something in the house was indeed making itself known.

Brian was new to the job and new to the 'community' at Newstead. A test? Perhaps. Or had this new employee found himself in the wrong place at the wrong time?

Things have been seen in the Cloisters - the shade of a woman garbed in black. Might Brian have encountered such a thing by accident? And, more pertinent, could his journey from the West Tower to the Cloisters have any bearing?

Dying canons were conveyed to the Oratory, there to be comforted by services taking place in the adjacent church during their last days. From here they would be borne to their place of final rest beneath the Cloister's flagstones - their ignominious rest twice disturbed by the Byrons' 5th and 6th Lord.

Remember: *'But choose a form - in that we will appear'?*

"The Oratory," Byron says, sipping wine poured by Joe Murray. "That room raises past spectres, Joe. Painful memories of something that occurred when I was a boy."

"I don't recall, sir?" A prompt from Joe though he is partly aware of that to which his master alludes. He returns the decanter to the table.

"Think, Joe, youth does not prevent exposure to depravity."

"'Tis best forgotten, sir."

"Aye, good friend, you are right."

Yet Lord Byron is put upon to forever retain disagreeable memories alongside good. He picks up a pistol, absently aiming it at the door as he hears(?) the slow tread of the predator who violated his young years.

IV

The Byrons' - Mother and son - relationship with Lord Grey de Ruthyn, ambiguous at best, added further complications.

In his twenties, Lord de Ruthyn soon charmed both of them, Catherine, many years his senior nevertheless infatuated with his affability. However, de Ruthyn did not respond, the true object of his attention being the young Lord.

Byron's visits to Newstead abruptly ceased and in the summer of 1804, when de Ruthyn visited the family at Burgage Manor in nearby Southwell, Byron refused to remain in the same room as their guest. There is little doubt that on Byron's last visit to Newstead the enigmatic and reptilian de Ruthyn made unwelcome sexual advances towards him which so disturbed the boy it caused him to flee. In a letter dated 21st October, 1804, he told his half-sister, Augusta: '...*I have a particular reason for disliking him.*'

It is also possible that heated exchanges took place concerning Catherine's increasing obsession with Grey de Ruthyn which likely affected the stormy, yet peculiarly vital relationship between mother and son.

Byron's friend Hobhouse wrote: '...*an intimacy has sprung up between Byron and his noble tenant. And a circumstance occurred during* [this] *intimacy which certainly had an effect on his future morals.*'

A few years later, on the 7th August 1808, Byron himself wrote to Grey de Ruthyn: '*Your Lordship must be perfectly aware of the very peculiar reasons that induced me to adopt a line of conduct which however painful, and painful to me it certainly was, became unavoidable -'.*

To this Grey de Ruthyn replied: '...*I need not say to you who know I have not the power to command my feelings when...wounded what my sensations were.*'

Byron shudders, pours more wine and gazes absently beyond Joe.

"My lord -?" Joe is alarmed at Byron's sudden pallor, his obvious agitation.

"I charge you, Joe, it is nothing. Question me no further."

"Then please to put the pistol down, sir." Joe, too, is agitated and glances around nervously. "For a second there I thought we'd been joined by summat else."

Byron glances up from where he is sitting. "So you do acknowledge such things?"

Nanny Smith, fascinated by Joe's hopefully impending revelations, still hovers in silence.

Before Joe can answer, Byron says: "Do you not consider that this house offers a welcome? Talk of darkness is but a reflection of our own disturbing thoughts, and thus not always conducive. Let us be done with it. Allow it to act as saviour, more than devilish temptation..."

A sad grin invested with a dark humour creases the poet's face, as he conjures heaven and the abyss - the highs and lows of a disparate life. More subdued, he states, "The next step may be fatal. In this one plunge...Earth take these atoms!...The mountains whirl spinning around me - I grow blind. No. No! It cannot be, not yet. A fatal step is beyond contemplation."

Nanny Smith and Joe are obviously concerned by the master's outburst yet say nothing, powerless to do anything even if they should think it.

"Place your foot here," Byron continues, unseeing, his mind elsewhere. "- here, take this staff, and cling a moment to that shrub - now give me your hand..."

The somewhat disjointed reflection over, though the words are committed to memory, Byron feels he glimpses the future once more: a vision of a man up high, even as he himself is raised to the heights only to have thoughts and ideals dashed so cruelly on to the rocks of indifference.

V

The roof above the old nursery is a mess of angles, pierced by dormers and massive chimneys. There is no easy way along it, just a heart-stopping scramble on precipitous slates and over flues, often chest high. Any person venturing up there will court the knowledge that beyond the gully and the low crenellations at its edge is a drop of forty feet to the gravel of the Spanish Garden which waits to claim the unwary, reward a moment's carelessness.

This daunting prospect awaits Brian Ayres as he travels to work on a miserable, late-November morning in 1988.

At 7.30 a.m. true daylight is reluctant to dawn, muted by a sky as uncompromising as burnished steel washed with fine drizzle. Shapes hover, disappear, transmute in such mean, wretched days: days when bad things happen.

Brian senses the oppressive, absolute silence, broken intermittently by the melancholy drip of water from trees and guttering, the sudden cry of a water bird from a mist-shrouded lake. He shivers, alive to a sense of utter isolation. Darkened windows prompt the unsettling notion of someone studying, watching...But from an ostensibly empty building?

He glances uneasily at the roof, musters his resources, very aware its inspection cannot be delayed.

"It doesn't help when you don't like heights," Brian smiles wryly. "But it's necessary to keep the roof clear of debris, check that gutters remain unblocked. We find cartons, ring-pulls, and peacock feathers up there! If we don't do it, gutters overflow and rainwater finds a way into the House and onto the valuable contents. I love this job, but dread the rooftop trips."

His key rattles in the lock, interrupts the uneasy silence. Dull echoes of the closing door scurry into a hopefully unoccupied emptiness.

He'd set the alarms the night before so no-one could be in there.

He reaches for the light switches, only to pause, the air around him somehow restless.

"I knew straightaway that something was present but I couldn't see anything. It was as if whatever was there had waited for me.

"It's hard to describe. Just a presence. It's there, and you know instinctively *it's* watching you, but you can't see it.

"I felt uneasy, but knew I had to get on, but wherever I went that day whatever it was accompanied me. It was like having somebody by your shoulder constantly. In the end I just accepted it. At times it can be a bit lonely in here on your own but it clearly didn't mean me any harm.

"At eleven-thirty a.m., and unaccompanied, I climbed from the Orangery roof onto the still wet main roof. The slates were as slippery as ice. To get from one end of the roof to the other it's necessary to climb over a series of chimney flues about a metre and a half high, and like buttresses, and then scramble across a sloping roof. You can't wear gloves because you need the grip, so when it's cold your fingers soon grow numb."

It is wrong to underestimate what it took for Brian Ayers to make this journey, to clamber over cold, wet stonework and across greasy slates, too scared to look down.

"I climbed over the second flue and swung onto the next bit of roof, but as I did so my feet suddenly shot from under me. I was on my back and sliding down the roof, gully and crenellations racing towards me. They're not high enough to prevent me going over. I can clearly remember thinking: I'm about to get badly hurt.

"There's nothing to hang onto or grab, nothing to stop you. I didn't panic, there wasn't time."

Brian, unable to turn, careers down the steep pitch of the roof on his back, arms flailing, hands grasping, seeking a hold on anything to halt a sickening tumble. Speed is horrendous as he slithers, gaining velocity at every metre, the world a kaleidoscope of grass and gravel, shining slate and mud-coloured sandstone. And centrally, like the calm in the eye of a storm, his simple rationale - 'I'm going to get badly hurt' - quickly becomes his own acceptance of the inevitable.

'...here, take this staff and cling - now give me your hand...And hold fast my girdle'.

"Suddenly I seemed to be slowing. It felt like something was holding me back. I still slithered downwards but the impetus had lessened, though it didn't prevent me slamming into the stonework with an almighty thump. I was lying in the gully aware of this terrific pain lancing through my right leg. My jeans were torn and blood poured from a huge gash."

He still has the scar today.

Yet after all that his first thought turned out to be: *Bloody hell, look what I've done to my jeans!* "They were clean on. A perfectly good pair ruined.

"It appears my leg had shot through the gap between the crenellated stonework at the same time as my chest struck the upper part, causing me to bounce back into the gully. I was dazed, but when I finally regained my feet I discovered my chest wasn't even bruised. Then I noticed something strange - my anorak, shirt and tee shirt were all pulled up behind me, almost over my head. They couldn't have snagged on anything because there was nothing for them to snag on! It felt as though I'd been gripped by the collar, that someone had grabbed it to prevent my fall.

"I shouldn't be here today, probably not even alive. Afterwards the fire brigade tested the drop in dry weather with a life-sized dummy which went straight off the roof and down onto the garden, just as I could have done. After that we installed safety equipment up there."

So who, or what, prevented Brian's fall?

"I believe that whatever met me that morning sensed I was in danger. It never left me all that day, even after the accident, and I reckon it saved my life."

Thoughtfully, he adds: "I've never been frightened here. I think that there are things we don't understand in this house, but none are malicious. Most incidents happen in the first year or two of individuals starting work here. It's as if something wants to make contact with a new arrival, sort of get to know them. Whatever it is knows we care for the place, and in turn cares for us."

Despite earlier experiences, Brian Ayers remains

detached, even sceptical, and unimpressed by lurid tales at Newstead, many of which, he believes, are exaggerated. "Some are simply bunkum, others can be explained. Mind you, before I started working here I would have laughed had anyone told me what I'm telling you. *There is something different here. All of us who work in the place know it, and we've all had our experiences.*"

Byron blinks, passes a hand over his eyes: himself, Joe and Nanny Smith conscious of something having invaded their thoughts - names, dates, different locales, all from people who know and are attached to the place called Newstead.

"What strange fancies," Nanny Smith says, her voice muted, Byron and Joe unable to hear her.

Byron slides the wine decanter towards them. "Come friends, this is my last night here and I do not wish to depart on a melancholy note. Sit, share some wine, we can talk more on past times." He fills three glasses, then raises his own. "A toast to old times, to better times, to friends here, and others now departed..."

"Who've you got in mind, sir?" Joe wants to know.

"Why Joe, the best friend a man could have. One who lies close by."

Despite inheriting an often-saving sense of humour from his mother, Byron was victim to an overwhelming desire to love and be loved.

Hardly surprising then that in this situation he would seek solace in his devout love of animals, particularly his Newfoundland dog, *Boatswain*, a love which was returned in equal measure - *'beauty without vanity, strength without insolence, courage without ferocity, and all the virtues of man without his vices'.*

Nanny Smith smiles contemplatively. "I remember 'ow you would lie in a boat on the lake readin' and how, when you got tired of that, you'd roll into the water and that there big beast, Bos'n, would rescue you. Bless him, that hound would always sit waitin' on you on the bank."

"Such a loss, Nanny. Together with my mother, perhaps my two greatest losses. Life is a funny thing, my friends, it gives, it takes."

"You did him proud, m'lord." Joe hiccups and sets down his glass. "Beg pardon, sir. Aye, did him proud."

When Boatswain went mad and died in 1808, he was buried with great ceremony in a tomb on the site of the High Altar within the shadow of the derelict church. Grief stricken, Byron erected an imposing monument below which lies a vault containing three niches, each large enough to house a coffin. As Byron nursed a need to remain close to those he respected and loved, and somewhat disrespectful to his monastic predecessors, his Will of 1811 directed that he should be buried there alongside any heir, and his servant, Joe Murray.

"You refused a place alongside him, Joe," says Nanny Smith. "The master wanted you down there with him and that poor dog."

Joe sneers. "His lordship might be buried with dogs but I will be buried with Christians!"

Nanny retorts, "Then where will you lie when the time comes, Joe?"

"Ooh dunna you fret, woman, they'll find a spot for me either 'ere, or close enough by."

IN HONOUR OF THE DEAD

"Did you see that?" The labourer sounded incredulous.

Carrying out a routine inspection in the Abbey's Boiler House, he'd aimed the question at Brian Ayers.

"What?" Brian sounded irritated, impatient to proceed with his own duties.

The labourer hesitated then gestured. "Something in that doorway over there."

Not again, thought Brian obliged to ask, "What sort of thing?"

A head scratch, a shrug. "I don't really know. Like a shadow, only there for a second or so. I thought someone was standing there."

Brian saw little point in acknowledging whatever the man had seen, it being so insubstantial, so infuriatingly brief.

The Abbey's maze of rooms, passages and hidden staircases lead to less frequented areas, and leave one fairly certain that some are not completely devoid of occupation.

The Boiler Room is no exception, for something does walk this inhospitable place with its cold, flagged floors, vaulted roof and surgical cream paintwork. So many have seen it and attest to it, nor can it be dismissed as a trick of light.

A dark shape flits by a doorway in the wall built recently across the Boiler House. It remains only for a second and is gone, leaving one to wonder what did happen here to infuse the area with melancholy, and alternatively make it alluring.

This room was once the Refectory where the religious order partook of meals, enjoyed respite, engaged in discourse. Since then, a doorway from the Cloisters, and a second one leading outside have been blocked off. Floors have been raised, new walls erected, and new doorways opened up effectively changing the appearance and original plan.

What is this shape? A remnant from those earlier days? Perhaps someone in panicked flight hurrying across the room between openings which once existed? A revenant carrying the vestige of a memory so terrible that such emotions have become ingrained in the very stone.

There is, however, a less macabre possibility...

More than likely it is Joe Murray, reluctant to depart the place he knew and loved. A colourful, determined character, once a cabin boy in the navy, and latterly 'commissioned' to run the 5th Lord's 'navy'. A man who, after Devil Byron's demise, became a valued and trusted friend to the 6th Lord, and eventually to Colonel Thomas Wildman, the former school friend of Byron's, who purchased Newstead in 1817 for £94,000.

Born in 1760, Joe Murray was 86 when he died, an achievement in those times. Healthy to a fault, his health quickly deteriorated after he sustained an injury whilst chopping wood for the fires.

Newstead's longest serving retainer, Joe Murray resided there since being 16, apart from a brief, miserable period in service to the Duke of Leeds during the poet Lord's minority.

Returned to Newstead, he attained the position of Head Butler, but never allowed this status to interfere with his enjoyment. He appeared always neat in dress, was always conscientious despite a taste for beer aided by the custom that required the Head Butler to brew beer for the household, only table wines being bought in.

Joe relished evenings spent in his favourite chair by the fire in the servants' quarters. Glass in hand, he would regale all with his repertoire of bawdy songs, much to the distress of Nanny Smith who feared for the morals of the young, and impressionable serving wenches. Undaunted by her disapproval, Joe's songs became louder, their lyrics more lewd as the hour grew late.

Despite it, Joe's successive masters held the deepest respect for him, none more than Thomas Wildman. When Wildman decided to convert the old Refectory into a Servants' Hall, he consulted Joe who quite understandably enthused over the project.

Joe would picture himself at the head of the Hall's great table, surrounded and respected by other servants. He was their supervisor, soon to have his own domain, a place where he could rule.

Anxious to take his rightful place as soon as possible, he rose early every morning to check that the builders had started work, berating any who turned up late. At every opportunity during the working day Joe would return to supervise the work.

To attain his envious age - in those days life expectancy would be generally less than half his eighty six years - Joe must have enjoyed legendary health, rising early, usually half dressed, and in all weathers.

This could well have been the secret of his robust constitution.

But after the splinter deprived him of his sight, it was as though a bubble had burst. Joe quickly deteriorated, his humour vanished, and he pined away, the rude health he had enjoyed suddenly a thing of the past.

Wildman, attentive and kind as ever, attempted to cajole him: "Come, come, old boy, be of good cheer; you will yet take your place in the servants hall."

Joe refused to be consoled. "Nay, nay, sir," he replied, "I did hope once that I should live to see it finished, and take my seat at the head of it. I looked forward to it with some pride; I confess; but it is all over with me now, I shall soon go home."

Joe Murray passed away and lies buried in Hucknall Church close to the Byron vault. A sad end(?) for such a well-liked figure.

Joe had 'haunted' the soon-to-be Servants' Hall, harassing its builders. It is likely he still does. It is his kingdom wherein he seeks his place at the table's head. Such a formidable figure would hardly let go easily, his devotion to the Abbey and its owners eclipsing even death.

He told Thomas Wildman he would 'Soon go home'. He certainly did and remained in the only home he had known for seventy years, the place where he truly belonged.

A *'Shadow! or Spirit! ...return'd to the earth...'*

Byron addresses Joe. "It is good that you will remain here, my trusted friend, and ... " He turns to Nanny

Smith, "... it saddens me that I shall leave you both but be assured I will share your expectations.

"As it is I must take my leave of you." He glances at, then beyond them, loathe to depart the home he loves. "I am grieved beyond measure as I am by the certainty we shall never meet in this life again."

A sigh lingers. "My heart is torn by one other parting..." It tails off, further deep sorrow evident.

"There is another matter over which I beg you to remain silent. You are both doubtless aware of my feelings for my sister, Augusta, the one person who remains most dear to me. You will have noted our close attachment, our intimacy. I ask you to swear on my mother's grave never to divulge what you may have witnessed to a living soul."

The two servants exchange glances, before Nanny Smith assures, "You may depend on our discretion, sir. Joe and me will carry our thoughts to the grave."

Joe nods his agreement.

VII

His life and expectations in tatters, and dogged by press and contemporaries alike, Byron saw no other recourse than to depart England a second time.

With little hope of reconciliation with Annabella, and troubled by an increasing persecution complex, might he have yearned for Newstead's tranquillity, perhaps to return one last time to contemplate his past, his present and an uncertain future? And take with him his half-sister, Augusta Leigh?

From corridors of the mind, this lonely man stares through windows, to see the shade of the still small boy he had been, half limping, half running to embrace his home, as ravaged by time then as it still is.

'A mighty window, hollow in the centre,
Shorn of its glass of a thousand colourings,
Through which the deepened glories once could enter,
Streaming from the sun like seraph's wings,
Now yawns all desolate.'

Shunned, publicly reviled, virtually friendless, and as desolate as the ruins he contemplates, Byron turns to his beloved Augusta about whom he wrote: *'There is not a more angelic creature on earth'*.

Close from childhood, their relationship intensified in maturity.

'She was like me in lineaments - her eyes, Her hair, her features, all, to the very tone Even of her voice, they said were like to mine; but soften'd all, and temper'd into beauty.'

Augusta, neglected by her race-loving, spendthrift husband, received monetary gifts from Byron for herself and her children. No stranger to Newstead, she once joined him there two years earlier, winter snow detaining them for some weeks. Rumour hinted that they had committed incest and it has been suggested that Augusta's daughter, Medora, was Byron's child, although there is little or no evidence to substantiate this.

Afterwards, Byron's writings do perhaps lend some credence to it, when he says in Manfred Act II: *'...it were the deadliest sin to love as we have loved.'*

It is also reinforced by a confession, which Augusta purportedly made in confidence to Byron's wife Annabella, after Byron had left these shores. Spiteful as ever, Annabella lost little time in using her well-trained band of attendant, inveterate gossips to spread the news. She even used and adopted Medora who, it appears, was even more grasping and deceitful than her mentor - and despite insinuations bore a striking resemblance to Augusta's husband, Colonel George Leigh - to inflict pain on her own unfortunate mother.

After bitter-sweet remembrance of days spent with Augusta, walking in the grove above the Abbey, in Devil's Wood, and carving a permanent proclamation - 'Byron' and 'Augusta'- on a twinned stemmed elm, Byron's destiny drove him to embark on his chosen journey. A parting this painful from two great loves in his life prompted the following lines from 'Epistle':

'Go where I will, to me thou art the same -
A loved regret which I would not resign.
There are yet two things in my destiny -
A world to roam through, and a home with thee.'

Byron departed England on the 25th April, 1816.
Childe Harold resumed his pilgrimage.

CHAPTER SIX

SEPARATION

--oOo--

I

The bedchamber is cold, a weak sun filters through the drapes, the atmosphere made more tangible by the dust motes dancing in its rays.

A low groan issues from beyond the closed door and the wind buffets a nearby casement, interrupting sleep.

Byron rises groggily. "What's that? Speak if you have ought to tell me." He stumbles to the mirror - the grey-black mirror which reflects a different image.

Vast corridors and doors beckon in this house of many rooms, perhaps likened to the maze of his own memories, of things done, of others left undone.

"What do I see?" He leans forward but no breath frosts the mirror. "I departed, yet still linger, so tell me of my life...What is it I wish to see...Again?"

He thinks again of Shakespeare. *'What beck'ning ghost...?'*

Across the lake... *'...the lucid lake, Broad as transparent, deep and freshly fed...'* Through the trees...Diadem Hill...A couple lying in the grass. Mary...

'I cannot marry that lame boy!' The skull cup brimming full... "Come, taste my wine."

'Away, away! There's blood upon the brim!' Pistol cracks rent the air...a hole punctured in the panelling... Laughing...Wenches scream their pleasure... Lucy again... "I won't believe you love me..." Her words fade, overtaken by chanting. A line of thirteen walk shadowed corridors...A wolf howls...A bear growls...Hobhouse, the others all jeering; wine drips, stains the floor...Then Caroline Lamb threatening suicide...Annabella sneering... *Insanity!* Skulls grin... "And drew from wither'd bones, and skulls, and heap'd up dust, conclusions most forbidden."

Dead and living rise to mock...Only Augusta reaches forth her hand...He needs to grasp it, to be pulled back...It remains elusive...

"Used. Used by you all...except Augusta. Perhaps it was only she who really understood. She and the Countess Guiccioli.

"When did it start? At school? An education in so many things. Is that why I submitted to you so easily May Gray, when you bade me be your true young master? But at least you did show me the right path from which even that queer Grey de Ruthyn failed to divert me.

"Oh those selfish, wanton bitches who later threw themselves at me. Why? Penniless me, what could they want other than to know what sexual congress with a cripple might offer? Women! Moulded in the devil's furnace and brought forth to torment man!

"All but you, sweet Augusta, the one port to which I cannot sail. I hold you, I kiss your lips, I reach...NO. NO! Too much! There lies torture!"

A tear falls but fails to moisten the inlaid leather of the desk.

"Augusta, how then can I exist without you?"

The room temperature falls. He turns, aware of - "What...what is this? A dark figure with no face beneath its drab, dark cowl."

A pale, almost skeletal hand beckons...towards the future. Byron reaches. What else is there?

Ah, the servants have changed their attire. They walk the halls as before, they clean, they show humour, so amusing to see them pause as though noticing something, only to shake their heads thinking it whim, or fancy. Yet as they depart they look back over their shoulders. They never change, the pretty, flighty ones, the dour, dried-up matrons, all feeling a slight unease.

He knows this room with its view across the Lake. It is in the West Tower hidden away up a short flight of stone steps lit by a stained glass window. In his typical theatrical way Byron chose the room, notwithstanding its close proximity to the Prior's Oratory and that room's unsavoury connections. Indeed, the Oratory afforded him useful dressing quarters.

The bedroom itself is not exceptionally large and houses other effects and artifacts belonging to the poet. Whilst the building enjoys a peace and tranquillity rarely shared by many such great houses in the area, each of its rooms contain their own autonomous peculiarities, this room being no exception.

A young woman enters. "Here my pretty, let me stroke your cheek." Byron whispers a name, heard from somewhere when he had walked the house on another occasion. He reaches to touch the pretty face before him...

Patricia Davis, a fairly tall, vivacious young woman, and guide, loves it up here. "People don't always want to come up and turn off the lights, but I will. It doesn't bother me at all."

This, despite what many might consider a shattering experience in that same room.

Tricia, in carefree mood, opened up Byron's bedroom, blithely pulling back curtains and lifting blinds when, out of nowhere and by her shoulder she heard a voice: "Patricia!" She spun round to find the room empty.

"My name was whispered. 'Patricia' not Tricia which I prefer...but Patricia. There was no intonation of any kind, and it was very close, within a foot or so of my ear. There was no-one else up here. I wouldn't say I was frightened, though my heart was thumping, more from shock than anything else.

"Apart from that, it's been the odd noise, or like a feeling of being touched. By that I mean my hair stroked, or a hand brushed gently against my cheek. But these were never as strong as what happened in Byron's bedroom, or in the Library."

So many tales are rife of things encountered here; of shapes glimpsed in the mirror sited above the coffin stones which later formed the fireplace mantle; tales of workmen who have fled, refusing to return.

GRAVE IMAGES

He contemplates further lines already written.

'Think'st thou existence doth depend on time? It doth; but actions are our epochs: mine have made my days and nights imperishable, endless, and all alike, as sands on the shore.'

Another woman bustles in.

In his eyes, a dried-up matron to all intents. Devilment enters the equation. "I'll have you knock before you enter here, madam. You will not treat me the way you treat your minions!"

Jean Price, wife of Sam Price, the former Head Caretaker, is said to have been a formidable woman who reputedly terrorised the housekeeping staff, but ironically came to be terrorised herself.

This singular incident lends belief that Newstead repays in kind: contrary to the experience of someone as personable as Tricia Davis, Jean Price is taught a lesson.

Said to be abrasive and unpleasant to those of whom she had charge, Jean Price's treatment would be more dreadful than any she had meted out.

In the course of her duties, and as she had so often done before, Mrs. Price made her way to Byron's bedroom to ensure, in her words that 'not a speck of dust was present'.

With typical fastidiousness, and so intent upon her inspection, she slowly became aware that something was awry. The room itself seemed to breathe a different, more chilling intent, and abruptly ceased to be the room she knew and cared for.

Did Jean Price's forbidding demeanour also disturb past echoes? A long forgotten reaction from someone who recognised and was appalled by her temperament?

This subtle atmospheric change in Byron's bedroom preceded the abnormal, inexplicable sounds of disembodied breathing. Jean instantly stopped her labours to anxiously glance about her vainly seeking a source. To her amazement, and mounting fear, she failed to discover any cause. Her agitation increased as the sounds refused to be pinpointed. Finally, her composure shattered and in absolute terror she took flight, promising to never enter the room again, not even to collect her dusters and polish.

Despite all the confusion, Byron again seeks the mirror.

He is here, yet he is not. But what brought him back? "I am Childe Harold, so where did I resume my pilgrimage?"

II

He landed at Ostend, and accompanied by a young physician, John William Polidori and faithful servant, William Fletcher, he crossed Europe.

Despite prolonged travelling, a real home proved elusive - Newstead still uppermost in his thoughts. In truth, he found no other home *to fix his heart upon'.* In May, he reached Lake Léman where he rented the Villa Diodati. Here he met Percy Bysshe Shelley who had arrived a few weeks earlier accompanied by his wife Mary and her step-sister, Claire Clairmont, already pregnant with Byron's child after their brief liaison in London shortly before his departure.

Therefore did unwanted spectres, which had accompanied him from England, find embodiment in his tale *The Vampyre*, Byron's somewhat reluctant contribution to the now well-documented ghost story evening at the Villa Diodati suggested by Mary Shelley?

In this tale, Lord Byron tells of a blue-blooded aristocrat from an ancient family called Darvell. Might this character have been drawn on the very personage of *Devil* Byron?

This story, curtailed by Byron, was eventually resurrected back in London by Polidori, who had rewritten and expanded it during two or three idle mornings in that summer of 1816, when Byron and Shelley were otherwise engaged in discourse, or sailing on the vast lake. In yet another analogy, Polidori turned the poetic Darvell into villainous Lord Ruthven, a satire on Byron himself, described by Caroline Lamb as 'mad, bad, and dangerous to know'.

This mirrors Lady Caroline Lamb's novel *Glenarvon*, penned in the same year. Here she revenged herself on Byron, her arrogant, if stylish, former lover, in her creation of the satanic Clarence de Ruthven, Lord Glenarvon.

Polidori's re-vamped vampire returns from Turkey to prey on London society. The story became an instant best seller, partly because everyone assumed it was written by Byron himself.

Interestingly, did Grey de Ruthyn, the lessee of Newstead during Byron's minority, provide the inspiration for the predatory Lord Ruthven, given that de Ruthyn had made unwelcome advances to Byron's mother, Catherine, and the young lord himself?

Could this confidence have been betrayed by an embittered Caroline Lamb?

By 1822, despite the loss of his illegitimate daughter, Allegra - sent to him by Claire Clairmont in 1817 - and the final loss of Newstead to his old friend Colonel Thomas Wildman, Byron's state of mind improved. His writing became more prolific, his journeying more intense, and presumably enjoyable. Perhaps travel had proved to be an opiate, relieving the pain of separation, or becoming a successful means by which he could lay his own ghosts.

When he departed England in 1816, he wrote: *'In England the only homage they pay to virtue is hypocrisy.'* A year later Byron was able to write: *'England! With all thy faults, I love thee still!'* Perpetual motion may have relieved the symptoms, but it was by no means a cure.

In 1819, Byron's old friend Tom Moore, the poet, visited him in Venice. He wrote that he (Byron): *'...had grown fatter, both in person, and in face, and the latter had suffered most by the change, having lost, by the enlargement of the features, some of that refined and spiritualised look that had in other times distinguished it, but although less romantic, he appeared more humorous.'*

In the summer of 1821, Shelley visited Byron at Ravenna and remarked that: *'Lord B. is greatly improved in every respect - in genius, in temper, in moral views, in health and in happiness...He lives in considerable splendour, but within his income...'*

Despite this, Byron nursed an almost overwhelming desire for rehabilitation back in England, finally assuaged in 1822 when he eventually settled in Genoa at Casa Saluzzo with Countess Guiccioli whom he had first met in the spring of 1819.

Attracted to the Countess, Byron took pleasure in her company. He had escorted her to La Mira in Venice, where he scandalised the neighbourhood by living with her until her indignant, sixty-year old nobleman husband appeared. Like most of his relationships, Byron grew tired, but the Countess would unfortunately prove singularly difficult to shake off.

She had, he discovered, *'awful notions of constancy'*.

One year later, Lady Blessington visited from England and commented, *'melancholy was his prevailing expression'*. Initially, she was disparaging; he dressed in over-decorated, unfashionable, cheap clothing that did not fit, but gradually she was won over. She wrote: *'...it is impossible not to observe how tender and affectionate a heart his must have been, ere circumstances had soured it'*.

Byron's clothes were ill-fitting because, since Tom Moore's visit, the poet had lost weight. Was it entirely due to his dietary regime, or the myriad *new* problems that beset him?

The Pope had dissolved the marriage of Countess Guiccioli, and she and her ageing father, Count Gamba, were now installed with Byron at the Casa Saluzzo.

Then came Leigh Hunt whom Shelley had invited to Italy after taking seriously the light-hearted suggestion by Byron that the three could edit a radical magazine from that location which could be ultimately purchased in London. The venture was unsuccessful, but after Shelley's departure and subsequent death in a boating accident when his yacht *Ariel* capsized in a storm off the coast of Italy, Byron unwillingly assumed responsibility, both financial and otherwise, for Leigh Hunt, his wife, and their six children.

Maybe Byron recalled his own years of poverty and the invaluable support of friends like Scrope Davies. The responsibility was, however, unwelcome; at this time he was gathering all his resources for his impending departure to Greece.

To compound this, Mary Shelley, who had remained in Italy after her husband's death, appeared in June. She and Byron disliked each other, but now she needed money to pay for her own return to England and applied to Byron indirectly through Leigh Hunt.

Byron and Leigh Hunt had very little in common; they argued, although Byron still kept the Hunt family until they finally departed Genoa in 1823. Contrarily, he did not pay for Mary Shelley's journey.

Add to this the growing conviction that his literary popularity was over, Byron's dark mood prompted, "I am the most unpopular writer going." And: "My day is over, **Vixi**."

Despite all, he remained convinced that his current work was superior to anything he had earlier produced. He had resumed work on *Don Juan*, earlier laid aside at the request of La Guiccioli, and was once more pouring out the successive cantos of a masterpiece for which he did not expect to receive public acclaim, but was determined to *'not willingly let die.'*

By 1823 he was desperate to escape complications and household trivia. The cause of Greek independence from the Turks apparently offered an ideal solution. The idea that the birthplace of democracy should be returned to its rightful owners had gripped intellectuals, the literati and press alike in England. These were the people Byron needed if he were to achieve longed-for rehabilitation.

With typical impetuosity he flung himself, and his money, into the horrendous complications of the cause, corresponding with the Greek Committee in London to further his aims.

Only when it appeared too late to extricate himself did doubts surface. He learned that the Greeks themselves were divided, the opposing factions in-fighting when they were not in conflict with the Turks. Nor did the Greek Committee in London offer assistance, being just as disorganised. Plagued with self-doubt, Byron realised too late that he was committed.

He told Lady Blessington: "It is not pleasant that my eyes should never open to the folly of the undertakings passion prompts me to engage in, until I am so far embarked that retreat (at least with honour) is impossible..."

To further complicate matters he had inherited an unshakable belief in prophecies and forebodings, and had been heard to say: "No consideration can induce me to undertake anything on a Friday or a Sunday."

Mrs. Williams' warning to Catherine Byron that her son should beware his thirty-seventh year, now fast approaching, may not have been far from his thoughts. Nor would the uncomfortable realisation that his own father had died at the age of thirty-six.

A further, and perhaps more profound comment to Lady Blessington, turned out to be prophetic and, as the world would learn to its discomfort, entirely accurate. He said: "You will think me more superstitious than ever, when I tell you that I have a presentiment that I shall die in Greece."

Synonymous with courage and generosity, as well as clear thinking, his name became an inspiration to the Greek rebels. But, as his prophecy had stated, the end was near.

As a doomed victim, sentenced to death, Byron, in defiance of all these portents, embarked on his journey on *Sunday, 13th* July, 1823.

He interrupted his journey, hesitating for some months on the Heptanesos Islands just off mainland Greece, in particular at Metaxata on the island of Cephalonia, before making the final crossing to Missolonghi where he arrived on 6th January, 1824.

Amidst its festering swamps, and only scant weeks after joining Prince Mavrocordato, Byron's health deteriorated.

Burning with fever, he found himself surrounded by incompetent doctors whose only remedy was to bleed an already weakened man.

'I tell thee, man! I have lived many years, many long years, but they are nothing now to those which I must number: ages - ages - space and eternity - and consciousness, with the fierce thirst of death - and still unslaked!'

On the 15th April he told them: "I will never consent to let you take an ounce of blood from me."

On the 16th, and too weak to offer resistance, he finally assented. Throwing out his arm he told them: "Come; you are, I see, a damned set of butchers; take away as much blood as you will; but have done with it."

Convinced he must die, in these final weeks he sought solace in more simple, innocent days spent at Newstead, and a face never forgotten:

'I have a passion for the name of "Mary",
For once it was a magic sound to me;
And still it here calls up the realms of fairy,
Where I beheld what never was to be;
All feelings changed, but this was last to vary,
A spell from which even yet I am not quite free'

Very sick, these reflections eased his discomfort, yet the future was ordained...

He stated to the attending Doctor Millingen: "Your efforts to preserve my life will be in vain. Die I must: I feel it. It's loss I do not lament; for to terminate my wearisome existence I came to Greece...One request let me make to you. Let not my body be hacked, or be sent to England. Here let my bones moulder. Lay me in the first corner without pomp or nonsense."

As he died, only incoherent mutterings could be heard, mere snatches of words, notably, "Augusta - Ada - Kinnaird - Hobhouse."

'To do this thy power must wake the dead, or lay me low with them. Do so - in any shape - in any hour - with any torture - so it be the last.'

Finally, at six in the evening on the 19th, he said, "I want to go to sleep now."

'He's gone - his soul hath ta'en its earthless flight - whither? I dread to think - but he is gone.'

Later that day Missolonghi echoed with the cry: *"Byron is dead."*

III

'I do not disbelieve that we may be two by some unconscious process...'

By two, do I mean the living and the dead? He muses.

By chance he does recall a passage contained in a letter he sent to John Murray dated 6th October 1820: *'In the latter end of 1811, I met...Peel...He told me that in 1810, he met me, as he thought, in St. James's Street, but we passed without speaking...it was impossible, I being then in Turkey. A day or two after, he pointed out to his brother a person on the opposite side of the way;* "There," *said he,* "is the man whom I took for Byron." : *his brother instantly answered,* "Why, it is Byron, and no-one else."

Nor was this the only time, thinks Byron and considers a further sighting of this so-called *doppelganger.*

"I was in bed delirious from a potentially fatal fever, many miles away at Patras in Turkey. *'If I had died there, this would have been a new ghost story for you.'*

So which of his 'two selves' is it, which falls prey to the surgeon's knife?

"I saw those butchers' blatantly ignore my final wishes and dissect my earthly remains. They removed internal organs as part of the embalming process, and yet I remain whole.

"What did they seek to achieve?"

'Still in my science - I can call the dead, and ask them what it is we dread to be...'

106

"Might it have been their morbid curiosity aligned to medicine's endless search to discover some observable manifestation, some clue to the source and mystery of life? Did they seek to uncover my genius? To capture the dying embers of my very essence?"

A doleful smile encapsulates the statement as he considers that when a 'source of life', like a candle is snuffed out, possibly it does still burn elsewhere.

A voice whispers: "Accept your fate for what it is; immured to walk these corridors of Newstead. For you and this house are one. Did you ever truly believe you could escape the diabolical acts performed by yourself and your illustrious ancestors? You must therefore accept that these have bound you to these sad, defiant stones."

Fatalistically, he does accept this, although when turning to discover the source there is no-one there.

Why then did they ignore his last wishes? Hadn't he said to Dr. Millingen: "...here [Greece] let my bones moulder..." ?

He had also intimated to his companion, Trelawny on the brig Hercules during his final crossing to Greece: "...there is a rocky islet off Maina - it is the Pirates' Isle; it suggested *The Corsair*. No one knows it: I'll show it to you on the way to the Morea. There is a spot I should like my bones to lie.

"Yet my earthly remains lie in a vault in the church of St. Mary Magdalene, Hucknall, and *I still linger* to attest to the fact."

"Ah," the voice interjects, "you believed that you possessed Newstead. Did it not occur to you that the opposite might be true? That you are possessed as so many before, and after you have been so possessed."

Byron's embalmed body had been placed, with separate earthenware jars containing his internal organs, in a packing case - the only thing resembling a coffin available. For two days an endless stream of people passed through the church at Missolonghi to pay their final respects before the state funeral held on the 22nd April.

A grisly postscript is contained in a deposition by the Greek authorities regarding the fate of the body. It states: *'...The lungs which are missing, were deposited, in deference to the repeated representations of the citizens of Missolonghi, in the church of San Spridione...'*

Despite his last wishes, the body, with his dogs, including a Newfoundland dog - a successor to *Boatswain* - were embarked on the brig 'Florida' under a salute from fortress guns, those same guns having thundered a Greek welcome such a short time before.

On 5th July, 1824, the 'Florida' anchored near London Bridge, Byron's body transferred to a lead coffin, its other contents to an urn. He lay in state at Sir Edward Knatchbull's house in Westminster for two days before the hearse undertook its slow journey to Nottingham.

Two final acts of spite awaited him. He was refused a revered place in Westminster Abbey and his widow, Annabella, would have nothing to do with the funeral arrangements. Nor did she attend his funeral, Augusta Leigh finally assuming responsibility.

"HIS ROOM WHERE I WAS ROOTED"

Annabella could, of course, no longer have felt anything for Byron, his final disposal being of no interest to her. Even so, there may be another explanation.

Byron, it can be recalled, had refused to take her to Newstead fearing that she would fall in love with the place. In 1818, after its sale to Thomas Wildman, she did visit. Her journal entry dated 22nd May, 1818, is enlightening. She wrote: '...*the apartments were in every respect the same...he might have walked in...the parapets and steps where he sat...the leads where he walked...his room where I was rooted having involuntarily returned...*'

Could these words be the nearest Annabella ever came to admitting her true feelings?

After all she had said and done, Annabella was perhaps afraid that in attending Byron's funeral the ice might yet melt and the tears flow. Or is there another explanation?

Love and hate - the opposite sides of the same coin and very closely aligned. Byron had refused to die in obscurity abroad, scorning the image of a ridiculous, aging Lothario hobbling after a succession of old crones. Instead, the man had died a hero, not in a romantic charge against blazing guns, yet as good as. In doing this, and much to the chagrin of contemporaries who still hated him, he became more popular than ever.

As for Annabella, had Byron not compounded her agony by requesting Lady Blessington's assistance in obtaining a copy of Annabella's portrait? This impressed the Lady in his favour, and effectively undermined Annabella's own efforts at self-justification. The only course left to her, and her like, would be to ignore this final upsurge of public adoration for Byron.

On its journey to Nottingham, and by some dramatic chance, Lady Caroline Lamb, still the wife of William Lamb, now Lord Melbourne, was suddenly confronted by the funeral cortège on the outskirts of London. This was ten years after their dramatic liaison, and as she turned her head on this summer's day, she had been apparently unaware of its significance until she learned later whom the coffin contained. The resulting shock became unbearable: she would never recover. She separated from her husband the next year and died a few years after.

Three months after Byron's death the coffin finally reached Nottingham.

Early on the morning of July 16th, large crowds watched it being taken along Fishergate, Cartergate, Hockley and up Carlton Street to the *Blackamoor's Head Inn* where it was mounted on trestles in a room at the north-west corner of the inn yard. Displayed at its head stood the casket containing the internal organs. The room, draped in black, had three escutcheons of the Byron arms fixed to all four walls. The mourners were allowed in twenty at a time.

Nearby, a carriage halted, its occupant intrigued by closed shops, by crowds flocking to the *Blackamoor's Head Inn,* and the otherwise deserted streets. The passenger urged her driver to enquire what was happening. A passer-by told him: "We are going to pay our last respects to Lord Byron whose body lies at the Inn." There followed a shriek from the carriage, its blinds quickly closed on the violently sobbing Mary Musters née Chaworth who, now almost hysterical with grief, was driven away.

At 11.45 a.m. a vast and silent procession - including Byron's friends Hobhouse and Hanson; Augusta's husband, George Leigh; Colonel Thomas Wildman, new owner of Newstead, and the Mayor and Corporation of Nottingham - proceeded to Hucknall.

Lord Broughton, another of Byron's friends, and executor, was the last person to shake Byron's hand when Byron left England in 1816. He described how the procession, a quarter of a mile long, wound its way through Papplewick and Linby, passing nearby Annesley Hill, immortalised by the poet and still 'crowned with its peculiar diadem of trees', to reach the village church so crowded it was difficult for the mourners to follow the coffin up the aisle.

Thus the errant genius was laid to rest at 4 p.m. in the vault to which his mother had been brought in 1811, and where he would be followed in 1852 by his daughter, Ada, after her death from uterine cancer.

It left one intriguing irony.

Could it have been mere coincidence that Byron, his father, and Ada all died at the age of 36? Or that Ada, despite her mother's efforts to alienate her from her father, chose to be buried alongside him?

Two years before her death, Ada paid her only visit to Newstead and became smitten, writing of it: *'My* first *& very melancholy impressions at Newstead, gradually changed to quite an* affection *for the place before I left it. I began to feel as if it were* an old home, - *& I left it with regret & reluctance, - & I feel that I* must *go back to it before the year is over.'*

Inheriting her father's sense of fatality, she had written in 1842: *'...there are the seeds of destruction within me. This I* know.*'*

Such dark seeds flourished and fed by wishes aired, had their final say. She would return, but not for more than two years. In death, Ada fulfilled her resolution, taking her desired place alongside her father in nearby Hucknall.

'Seek out - less often sought than found -
A soldier's grave, for thee the best;
Then look around, and choose thy ground,
And take thy Rest.'

Childe Harold had finally come home.

CHAPTER SEVEN

REALISATION

--oOo--

I

'And on thy head I pour the vial
Which doth devote thee to this trial;
Nor to slumber, nor to die,
Shall be in thy destiny;
Though thy death shall still seem near
To thy wish, but as a fear;
Lo! The spell now works around thee,
And the clankless chain hath bound thee;
O'er thy heart and brain together
Hath the word been pass'd - now whither!'

"Dead! Dead! That cannot be."

Aroused by a sudden realisation, even though he evades its truth, Byron hurries across the close-cropped lawns to fling himself upon the steps of Boatswain's tomb.

Might he not have sat here once before?

"Dead, surely not. You, dear friend, but not I." He caresses cold stone, very unsure. "Bos'n...BOS'N, do not ignore me now."

A Newfoundland dog gallops across the grass, hesitates momentarily, whimpers, then turning, dashes on towards a couple in earnest discussion on the edge of the woods beyond.

Byron's shout of, "Bos'n, why do you not acknowledge me?" dies in the breeze-blown air. Squinting, he peers again towards the distant figures. Recognition dawns. He shouts: "THOMAS! THOMAS WILDMAN...IT IS I..."

Ignorant of anything, the couple separate, and he sees Wildman and the great dog depart without acknowledgement.

The woman, dressed all in white, comes towards him. Augusta? Is it she? He waves hoping to draw her attention. She settles on the steps of the tomb.

He is irked by her indifference. "Good day to you, madam." He glances skywards. "The signs are good."

She remains impassive, his hackles rise. He then notices how close to her face she holds the writing slate she carries, how little she appears to be aware of her surroundings, or of the gardeners who carry on as though she were not there.

"Who are you?" He inquires.

Almost as though a breeze has caressed her, she looks up, sees nothing, and once again busies herself writing upon the slate.

Who is this woman?

II

Evidence establishes Newstead Abbey as a place where the supernatural is never far away. Spirits make their presence known, sometimes in disturbing ways. Why do they linger? If it is not simply recorded memory, do they, by their own will, insist on remaining? Or, do the stones of the building retain and often imbue them with a kind of half-life?

Edie Barker worked as a gardener at the Abbey in 1915, during its occupation by the Markham family. One of her duties was to collect the morning papers from the 6.30 a.m. train at Newstead Station while on her way to work.

On a bitter winter's morning Edie made her solitary journey along a deserted drive, pockets of mist clinging to the woods and hollows either side. To the east, the first faltering signs of day slowly delineated the horizon, the crunch of her boots on gravel her only known companion. Her solitude became more apparent as she neared the Abbey, its kitchen bereft of life, other than the everyday sounds of pans bubbling on stoves, of kettles whistling on hobs, all reminiscent of an abandoned 'Marie-Celeste'.

Unable to raise a reply to her shouts, Edie deposited the newspapers in their designated spot and turned to leave.

Reluctant to depart the captivating warmth on such a cold morning, she eventually made her way through nascent daylight to the women gardener's bothy situated behind the Stable Block adjacent to the Lake. Her mind on matters of the day, she stopped abruptly, aware of a human form glimpsed through the corner of her eye, which slowly seemed to materialize close to the water's edge.

In a breathy whisper, she uttered: "The White Lady."

Backing away, Edie turned and bolted like a terrified animal. "I ran like mad, nothing could have stopped me until I reached the bothy. All the while I was thinking: I hope there's somebody already at the bothy. I didn't fancy being there on my own with that...that thing roaming about outside.

"None of my workmates were surprised when I told them what I had seen. Since then others have asked me if I'm sure it was a ghost, and not a tree or something like it. Of course I was sure, having worked in the gardens long enough to know what all the bushes and trees look like!"

This was the only time Edie Barker saw the apparition of The White Lady, but it became an event, even after eighty years, which she could recount with clarity.

So who, or what, is The White Lady?

Thomas Wildman, walking in a gloomy grove close to the Abbey in 1823, noted a spectral figure of a woman quickly skipping from sight ahead. Soldier that he was, he refused to be alarmed. When, shortly after, he found a piece of her clothing, it confirmed his suspicions this was no phantom.

Wildman would deem himself fortunate: many like Edie Barker, who have since glimpsed Sophia Hyatt, have obviously seen what he discounted - her ghost.

Visitors to Newstead Abbey were not uncommon, especially since the time of his predecessor, the 6th Lord, but Wildman's curiosity was roused. He questioned the gardeners who told him it was the 'Little White Lady' who lived at the Weir Mill farmhouses in the skirts of the nearby woods.

"She comes to the Abbey every morning, keeps about it all day, and goes away at night," he was informed. "She speaks to nobody, and we are rather shy of her, for we don't know what to make of her."

She did visit every day, dressed in a white gown with a black bodice and a white hat with a short veil, but neither spoke to, nor even acknowledged anyone.

Sophia wandered the garden, avoided strangers, and would sit for hours beneath the tree upon which Byron and Augusta had carved their names, or at the foot of *Boatswain's* monument. She would read, or sometimes write on a small slate with a pencil, but more often she would be locked in hours-long reverie.

Legend has it that she was the granddaughter of the Honourable William Byron of Badwell Hall, a distant cousin of the 6th Lord. Her mother had married one of the estate's dog-keepers named Hyatt. William Byron disowned his daughter and, as a result, Sophia's parents were obliged to survive by selling books. She had two brothers, both of whom emigrated to America, one allowing her a small annuity after her parents' death, from the sale of their property.

Though she never met the 6th Lord, a bond formed, the obvious link, his poetry: this urged her to move to the district and closer to Byron's ancestral home.

A generous Wildman accepted her presence, but when his sister spent her honeymoon at the Abbey, an incident occurred which changed both his and Sophia's life.

Wandering the grounds, Wildman's sister happened upon Sophia. So great was her shock at seeing this pale figure drifting through the shadows of the grove close by the ruined church, that the sister took flight.

A distressed Sophia sent a note to Thomas Wildman saying how perturbed she had been by his sister's sudden retreat. She regretted the incident, upset at being an object of alarm. She explained how she idolised the poet, worshipped his genius, and nursed a solitary passion for haunting the places where he had lived. She went on to say that she was bereaved, alone in the world, and hinted at social infirmities serving to isolate her from others.

So desolate was her life that she hoped Wildman would continue to allow her sojourns in the gardens.

Wildman did consent, but upon visiting Weir Mill he unwittingly walked into the midst of an unfolding tragedy.

The woman he encountered appeared a sad figure approaching middle age, who struggled against adversity. Illness had robbed her of hearing; she was dumb, poorly sighted and plain in appearance.

They conversed by writing on a slate by which means she acquainted Wildman with her situation, Wildman coming to understand how utterly lonely and friendless she had become. Due to her misfortunes and infirmities, she lacked the power of social intercourse and quite understandably she brooded, her eccentricity forging apprehension in others.

Naturally feeling excluded, she told Thomas Wildman: "I am always amongst strangers as so much in my native country as I could be in the remotest parts of the world. By all I am considered a stranger and an alien;

no-one will acknowledge any connection with me. I seem not to belong, nor to be regarded as belonging, to the human species."

Her infatuation for Byron who, unbeknownst to her, was making preparations for an enterprise that would end in tragedy, grew all-consuming. The following verse, penned by Sophia, encapsulates her disposition:

> *'Thine image haunteth me like a past vision;*
> *It hath enshrin'd itself in my heart's core:*
> *'Tis my soul's soul - it fills the whole creation.'*

Yet, even this pathetic existence would be preferable to that which approached.

First, her beloved Byron's heroic death in Greece, and his eventual coming home to be buried nearby, would bring Sophia, as one of thousands of mourners, to see him laid to rest. It prompted:

> *'Well thou art gone - but what wert thou to me?*
> *I never saw thee - never heard thy voice -*
> *Yet my soul seem'd to claim affiance with thee.'*

Now, no-one else could command his affection; in her mind he was hers alone to adore and venerate. In turn she could never be free of either Byron or Newstead. Initially, she may have hoped the poet would return, that they would meet, and a special spark ignite a fire hot enough to weld their hearts forever. At his loss, Sophia sought comfort at the place he had grown to love.

Boatswain's tomb became her altar, and when a Newfoundland dog - Boatswain's successor, brought back from Greece and adopted by Wildman - re-appeared on the grounds, the two struck up an immediate friendship, Sophia looking upon it as living contact with her idol.

Slightly uplifted, her spirits were further dashed when her annuity abruptly ceased. Her brother's sudden death in the West Indies had thrown his affairs into confusion, and Sophia was forced to exist on the goodwill of a distant cousin who made her a tiny allowance. For five months Wildman made use of his contacts in the Caribbean in an attempt to unravel what was happening, to no avail.

Sophia's circumstances grew steadily more desperate, prompting her decision to travel to London and engage a lawyer who could attempt a sorting out. Whilst making her preparations she again resorted to verse:

'Farewell to thee, Newstead, thy time riven towers
Shall meet the fond gaze of the pilgrim no more,
No more may she roam through thy walls and thy
bowers,
Nor muse in thy cloisters at eve's pensive hour.

Oh, how shall I leave you, ye hills and ye dales,
Where lost in sad musing, though sad not unblest
A lone pilgrim I stray - Ah! In these lovely vales
I hoped, vainly hoped that the pilgrim might rest.'

On the 19th September, 1825 Sophia Hyatt made her last, poignant visit to the Abbey, there to linger at every place associated with Byron. As a last gesture she placed a sealed packet in Louisa Wildman's hands and begged her not to open it until after her departure for London. With that she bid a tearful farewell.

That evening, contrary to Sophia's pleas, Louisa Wildman felt compelled to open the packet. Inside were a number of poems and a long letter detailing Sophia's desperate situation, which closed with the following words: 'May you never know the agony I endure in tearing myself from all that the world contains of [sic] dear and sacred to me - the only spot on earth where I can ever hope for peace or comfort!'

Louisa, so moved by this, showed it to her husband. Both terribly afraid of what might befall her, they agreed that Sophia must not be allowed to leave, and further, that Sophia would be found a place at Newstead. If necessary they would support her until the problems might be resolved.

The following morning Wildman sent a message to Weir Mill Farm only to discover that Sophia had already obtained a lift on a wagon bound for Nottingham, there to meet the London coach. Desperate, Louisa Wildman despatched a servant to fetch Sophia back, instructing him to 'ride like the wind'.

After a hellish ride the servant reached the outskirts of the city, his frustration increasing as pedestrians and traffic forced him to virtually walking pace. At the same time Sophia sought directions, her coach departure imminent.

As the messenger neared the 'May Pole Inn' from which the London coach departed, crowds blocked his way. Not wishing to let his mistress down, the man frantically elbowed a passage through a gathered throng who reluctantly parted to reveal a small bundle of what appeared to be dusty clothes lying in the road.

Poor, deaf, half-blind Sophia, miserable, feeling the effects of a sleepless night and confused by the bustle, had stepped into the path of a speeding horse and cart. It had been mercifully quick.

Torment ended, she was no longer compelled to contemplate her ultimate fear expressed in the letter to Louisa Wildman: 'I dare not look beyond the tomb, yet I cannot hope for peace before.'

Physically she had joined her icon - her body later confined in Hucknall churchyard scant distance from that of the poet.

In the metaphysical sense, Sophia Hyatt returned to Newstead, her unquiet spirit seen in quiet contemplation about the gardens, and in the grove to the north of the house where the twin-stemmed elm, inscribed by Byron and Augusta, once stood - in Devil's Wood.

Perhaps the reason why Sophia Hyatt lingers is echoed in a verse about her empty life:

> *'And here, beneath this lonely tree -*
> *Beneath the earth thy feet have press'd*
> *My dust shall sleep - once dear to thee*
> *These scenes - here may the wanderer rest.'*

Also contained in her letter to Louisa Wildman are these words: 'My only wish now, is for rest and peace - endless peace; - "For rest, but not to feel 'tis rest": but I cannot delude myself with the hope that such rest will be my lot. I feel an internal evidence, stronger than any arguments that reason or religion can enforce, that *I have within me that which is imperishable*...could I but find that rest and peace in the grave which I have never found on earth, *and I fear will be denied me there.'*

Yet one other accurate prediction connected to Newstead. But it is more, because it poses the question: Was it simply an accident? Or should we once again consider the darker side - might the Abbey have been reticent to let her go?

By whose will does Sophia Hyatt remain at Newstead? Similarly, by whose will did Ada Byron become entrapped a generation later?

What did compel Louisa Wildman to open that packet in direct contradiction to Sophia's express instructions? And what really caused Sophia to take that last, fatal step...?

There can be no happy ending, but we hope that which is imperishable has, by whatever means, found peace, indeed companionship, in Newstead's 'lovely vales'.

Or does the 'Little White Lady' still wander in the hope of meeting the one with whom 'her soul seem'd to claim affiance'...beyond the grave?

In Byron's thoughts? Certainly in his words: *'Bear what thou borest, the heart and the form, and the aspect thou worest redeem from the worm. Appear! - Appear! - Appear! Who sent thee there requires thee here!'*

Or might the levels dictated by time and space still separate them?

So near, yet so far.

Byron is bereft, unable to reach this affiliated soul.
He watches Wildman disappear amongst the trees and
whispers "Thomas, you too? Are you not my saviour in
keeping this, my home?
"I know you, remember you..."

III

'NEWSTEAD! Fast falling, once-resplendent dome!
Religion's shrine! repentant HENRY'S pride!
Of warriors, Monks and Dames the cloistered tomb,
Whose pensive shades around thy ruins glide.'

A few years before Wildman purchased the building
and lands, Charles Skinner Mathews, visitor and
opponent to bear and wolf in the days of 'The Order of
the Skull' had this to say of Newstead:
'There are two tiers of cloisters, with a variety of
cells and rooms about them which, though not inhabited,
nor in any habitable state, might easily be made so; and
many of the original rooms, among which is a fine stone
hall, are still in use. Of the Abbey church only one end
remains; and the old kitchen, with a long range of
apartments, is reduced to a heap of rubbish. Leading
from the Abbey to the modern part of the habitation is a
noble room, 70 feet in length, and 23 feet in breadth; but
every part of the house displays neglect and decay, save
those which the present lord has lately fitted up.'
This, then, was the enormity of the task Thomas
Wildman embarked upon.

Wildman, had been a soldier who had distinguished himself in the Peninsular wars and at the Battle of Waterloo, where he was aide-de-camp to the Marquis of Anglesey. He entered the army in 1808 in the 7th Hussars, and was in the retreat to Corunna.

He came from a wealthy family, and inherited a large, profitable estate in Jamaica. A street in the capital, Kingston, still bears the family name. The inheritance provided the resources which enabled him to repair and renew Newstead Abbey, including reviving its estate by planting groves and forests. Estimates placed his total expenditure in this venture at over £100,000 - a veritable fortune, especially in the mid-nineteenth century.

In civilian life Wildman became equerry to His Royal Highness, the Duke of Sussex, who spent many holidays at Newstead. In the Duke's honour Wildman commissioned the Sussex Tower.

From all accounts he was a kindly man, underlined in his retention of Joe Murray who was fifty-seven at this time. In addition, Nanny Smith had moved from her housekeeper's apartment in the Abbey to a 'rock house' in the grounds, which consisted of three cells cut into a sandstone face. Wildman, concerned at the effect of such privation on a person of Nanny Smith's age, later moved her and son, William, to a new farmhouse on the estate.

Wildman commenced construction of new lodges for estate workers, something continued by his successors, the Webb family. However, the improved accommodation did not meet with universal approval, Nanny Smith being no exception. She objected to the move on the grounds that the 'rock houses' were warmer in winter, and cooler in summer, than the designated 'new' abode.

Visitors to the Abbey also encountered a Newfoundland dog wandering the grounds; not *Boatswain* resurrected, but the dog that had accompanied Byron's body on the journey home, and allowed to live out its days in close proximity to its doting master.

Indeed, both spirits *may* have finally come home!

The faithful Joe Murray remained as butler to Thomas Wildman until Joe's death at the age of 86. Up to now, Joe had turned out half-dressed every morning in all weathers to partake of what he termed his 'air bath'.

If anyone assumed that with the passing of the 6th and last Lord the book would close on the Abbey's unique and mysterious nature; that it was in some way tied inextricably to the family and its eccentric members, they would be mistaken.

Wildman, a man not given to flights of fancy, would discover that strange, inexplicable occurrences still enveloped Newstead.

One moonlit night he heard a noise not dissimilar to a carriage passing in the distance. Opening the windows, he leaned out only to define the sound 'as a great, heavy roller being dragged along the gravel walks and terrace'. There was nothing visible. When he mentioned this to the gardener the following morning, the man denied that anyone had been working late, and categorically stated that 'the roller has been chained up'. Wildman despatched him to examine it, and yes, the roller had been moved in the night, but the gardener protested that 'no mortal hand could have done so.'

Wildman, with characteristic humour, said to the man, "I am glad to find I have a 'brownie' working for me." By this he meant a benign helper such as an elf or pixie.

He did have one further brush with the 'supernatural' when walking in the gardens with his architect, and the small, female figure dressed in white flitted by. The remnant of clothing discovered was declared by his staff to belong to 'The Little White Lady'.

As we have seen, not an apparition but Sophia Hyatt, the country bookseller's daughter whose fixation with Byron led her to wander the gardens during daylight hours.

The hard work by Thomas Wildman and his staff revived Newstead. Unfortunately, the money expended on it, together with income losses sustained in the West Indies, forced the sale of Newstead on Wildman's death in 1860 to William Frederick Webb.

Fortuitously, Thomas Wildman did have the foresight to preserve the documents, writings and memorabilia of Lord Byron for posterity - a task enthusiastically taken up by his successor.

IV

William Frederick Webb had his roots in Westwick, County Durham. A wealthy man having inherited properties in West Yorkshire and Lincolnshire from an uncle, he had spent several years in Africa where he had befriended the missionary and explorer, Doctor David Livingstone.

Having purchased Newstead, the Webb's closed it to the public and embarked upon further restoration by adding to and enhancing the work done by Wildman. They created new roads; improved drainage and water supply; installed gas lighting to the Abbey and built the lodges and gate-houses. An addition worthy of note is the Stable Block with its characteristic, very prominent tower which immediately draws the eye.

It is a credit to their creators that these additions are in sympathy with the original architecture and blend admirably with the overall effect.

After eighteen months, and due to public outcry, the Webbs re-opened the Abbey four days per week to visitors in groups of six. By this time, the house had become more of a public museum due to its Byronic connections.

Visitors' remarked that Mrs Emilia Jane Webb was *'...much less mistress in her own house than caretaker for the Byrons'* - yet she felt she owed it to Byron's admirers to care for the Abbey and its contents.

Instrumental in protecting the famous carving made by Byron and Augusta on the trunk of the twin-stemmed elm, when the tree became diseased she had it felled, the inscription then removed to be placed behind glass in the Abbey.

Meanwhile, William became involved in litigation to prevent the drive becoming a public road. In achieving this he preserved the old rights-of-way along with the park's special character. Through the gradual spread of industry - notably coal mining - the Webbs came to depend on its derived income due to the fall in agricultural revenue. Soon mining would encroach on Newstead and its surroundings.

The following extract from an article which appeared in the 'Hampshire Magazine' in 1884, offers a credible, if somewhat exaggerated picture of its effect'

'I gazed upon the dew-spangled pastures and the luxuriance of the noble "monarchs of the forest", invaded by the grimy dust and poisonous smoke from the chimneys of a flourishing Colliery! The footprints of Byron obliterated by a mob of colliers with faces as sooty as their minds and manners! The winding pathway through the copse supplanted by a handful of lawless ruffians, who have covered the spot with their unsightly dwellings. About 1200 men are employed in the Newstead Colliery - an institution of twelve years' date. Long rows of miners' dwellings - built of brick and smeared with smoke and coal dust - occupy this once beautiful glen. A babble of Irish, North country; Welsh and English languages used in the least elegant phraseology, pours forth from the foul-mouthed herd of females who verbally bespatter each other from door to door.'

Nearby Annesley Colliery was owned by John Charles Musters, grandson of Byron's rival, Jack Musters, who had married Mary Chaworth - yet another coincidence as mining at that same colliery threatens Newstead today.

Both William and Emilia Webb were formidable people: William stood six feet four and was one of the best swimmers Eton ever had. In Africa, his adventures nearly cost him his life on occasion - twice he nearly perished in the Kalahari Desert. On his return voyage from Africa he was horrified when the captain refused to stop for two Lascar seamen who had fallen overboard, and Webb leapt into the sea exclaiming, "Then perhaps the captain will stop for a passenger."

When the Webbs moved into Newstead Abbey they were immediately confronted by its haunted reputation. In the dead of night, maids had become afraid of an old, panelled bedroom in which, they insisted, a column of cold, white vapour rose from its centre. Emilia immediately selected this room as her own bedroom; adamant the vapour would never again appear. We do only have her word for that - others have witnessed it since!

Peculiarly, Mrs. Webb was impervious to the cold and found it difficult to appreciate its effect on others. The regime in the house was strict, children expected to behave impeccably, living with cold considered good for them. And because the heating system did not extend to the Nursery, they were expected to run around to keep warm! Hot water bottles were taboo, as were eider-down quilts, and fires in the grates. The daughters, even in the dead of winter, wore thin dresses. Cold baths were compulsory unless the freezing, night-time temperatures rendered their sponges rock hard.

One celebrated visitor to the Abbey was William's old friend, Dr. Livingstone. He stayed there with his daughter Agnes for eight months from September, 1864 until April 1865, during which time he completed his book on the Zambezi and its tributaries. The Webbs' hospitality and the solitude Livingstone found at Newstead made his stay comfortable.

It was later said by one Sir Harry Johnston that these months were: '...perhaps, all things considered, the eight happiest months of his [Livingstone's] life'.

Perhaps a little strangely, Livingstone took hardly any interest in Byron, his poetry or his life, not appreciative of the fact that Byron had disinterred the graves of monks.

He said of Byron, "...his character does not shine. It appears to have been horrid."

Mrs. A. Z. Fraser, youngest daughter of the Webbs', makes the point that Byron and Livingstone did have one thing in common - they both gave up their all, including their lives, to the idea of freeing a suffering people.

After Livingstone's death in Africa, Henry Morton Stanley, the American journalist who had 'found' the great man, also visited Newstead, on occasion sleeping in Livingstone's old room.

Both Livingstone and Stanley planted trees at Newstead during their respective visits, those trees surviving today.

When Emilia Webb became terminally ill, both she and William followed Livingstone back to Africa in the hope that the better climate might prolong her life. She died at Matysfontein, South Africa, in 1889, scant two months after their arrival. William remained in Africa after her death, dying at Luxor in Egypt ten years later. Thus, two more owners of Newstead ended their days in 'exile'.

Over Emilia Webb's grave at Weinberg Cemetery near Capetown, William erected a recumbent cross of the type found in the Cloisters at Newstead.

On the death of William, the Abbey passed to his daughter, Geraldine, who married Sir Herbert Chernside. She engaged in further restoration, ordering the ivy stripped from stonework and the re-pointing of the structure. A wall enclosing the Monks' garden was requested, and also the construction of a summer-house at the north end. She was also responsible for the upper storey of the buildings running from the West Front, and two new windows in the East Front.

Lady Chernside died in 1910, succeeded by her sister, Ethel, whose primary interest centred on the garden. Her permanent memorial is the Japanese Garden, said to be the only one in England to make Japanese visitors feel homesick.

Five years on the Abbey passed to Ethel's brother, Roderick Webb, who served as a Captain in the South African war and who leased the place to Sir Arthur Markham.

In yet another of those odd ironies which surround Newstead, both landlord and tenant died on the same day in 1917.

The author, Mrs. A.Z. Fraser, inherited the Abbey on the death of her brother, Roderick, and became the last of its owners to live there, residing in a small portion of the house on the east side.

The Byron influence still exerted its fascinating hold, Mrs Fraser adding to the already copious collection of relics amassed by the poet and his successors at Newstead. Another woman of principle, she insisted that, on her death, she should be buried with those less fortunate in the cemetery at Newstead Colliery Village.

After her death in 1925, Charles Ian Fraser, her son and heir, was compelled by death duties to sell the house to Sir Julian Cahn, who donated it to Nottingham Corporation, its present owners.

Over its long life, the Abbey had slowly but incessantly, acquired a unique and mysterious reputation, nurtured by a succession of eccentric, often outrageous residents.

The Webbs had, like Thomas Wildman, exercised a degree of scepticism, and from a practical viewpoint they soon realised that if they did nothing to curb persistent rumours of ghosts they would find difficulty in obtaining staff.

WOULD YOU WISH TO LINGER IN THE PLANTAGENET ROOM?

We remember when houses were poorly lit and full of shadows, their roads and pathways cloaked in darkness, the silence all-pervading. And here we have a place where darkness contains things which only the foolhardy would dare to confront.

Despite attempts to suppress them, stories still seep from the Abbeys' ancient stones...

Maids complained of a presence hanging over them, and would refuse to linger alone in certain rooms, although nothing was ever seen. So easy to dismiss these as simple imaginings, but we shall see that an identical presence still resides there today.

A group of servants were adamant they had sighted an apparition in the form of a woman which floated past them, causing a footman to faint. Reporting this to Lady Chernside they were told to say nothing, since if word spread, no-one would want to work at the Abbey.

Relatively easy to dismiss as a harmless prank, but we should consider a conversation between Nanny Smith and Washington Irving.

A young lady, cousin of the 6th Lord, while in her bedroom one night, saw a lady in white appear through one wall, cross the room, and disappear through the opposite wall. In the same conversation, Nanny Smith told how the Keeper's wife had reported seeing a figure in the Cloisters near the Chapel, and another in the garden near to the Lord's Well.

On a dark, winter morning during the First World War, we have read of the young girl delivering newspapers who took flight when she saw a 'little white lady' in a hollow near the waterfall.

Today Newstead, out of season, stands virtually empty except for its dedicated caretakers, its peacocks and water-fowl, the latter certainly in residence since the time of Thomas Wildman, and possibly before.

And, of course, still those whom we may not always see...

CHAPTER EIGHT

THE SEER

--oOo--

I

"So, my Lord," the voice interrupts, " do you not yet see how valuable your presence here becomes?"

Byron whispers, as though to himself, " It is all so different, so much changed. The buildings, the gardens: all so formal, less desolate. Perhaps it is something I may have thought long about myself had the money been to hand."

He surveys the scene. "Aye, you look so spruce, so becoming now."

"Surely you could never believe this house and its lands could survive without you; your will, and its need to regenerate."

Byron begins to realise the truth of...What? Conscience? Or can it really be some other presence forcing him to take stock of...truth?

The voice interrupts. "Walk with me now, and I will show you what man and science choose to ignore.

"Time here is a flexible commodity which bends and curves, and sometimes overlaps. It is a channel by which we may reveal things to those who truly belong."

Truly belong!

A telling phrase when applied to Newstead Abbey: people do *belong*. As do memories; snatches of the past, which incite, disturb, even cajole.

The Abbey entices a large and varied cross-section of the public. Some are ardent admirers of the poet and his works, others, drawn by curiosity to see, indeed taste its special atmosphere, and confront its somehow fearful reputation.

Visit over, the majority take away with them a pleasant, lingering memory, although others look upon the experience as bewildering.

"Consider the Abbey's mirrors, Lord Byron," intones the voice. "In Newstead we see reflections, merely an approximation of reality.

"One step can take any unsuspecting visitor through a frail barrier, which separates them from a different world wherein its occupants still live out their existence *ad infinitum.*

"I speak of what others choose to call ghosts, sir."

On a Newstead 'ghost walk', a party of up to forty, present-day 'ghost hunters' are led to the Library by Pauline Corby, dressed in suitable attire as befitted a Victorian house-keeper.

Shadows are lifted only partially by subdued illumination creating an illusion of how it was in earlier times before the benefit of modern lighting.

The Library's bookcases collect reflections, images of two heavy tables placed in the window recesses.

Around one of these are positioned four rosewood, red leather-upholstered chairs awaiting the visitor, weary after nearly two hours spent moving through the house.

On this night, unnoticed by Pauline as she guides her party, one of these four chairs is set slightly back from its original position.

Pauline explains the significance of the Byronic artefacts, and recounts supernatural events, which occur from time to time in this room. As she does, a lady seizes the opportunity to take the weight off her feet by sitting on this chair.

As the room empties, Pauline is detained by some of the party intrigued by her narrative - the discussion suddenly interrupted by an agitated man who gestures wildly in the direction of the seated lady.

"There's an old man on that chair, and he's trying to push that woman off!" The man demonstrates by thrusting out his palms. "Can't you say something to her?"

Pauline sees nothing other than the woman enjoying her rest. "I'm sorry," Pauline quizzes, "what does the man look like?"

"Surely you can see him." The man, frustrated, is conscious of puzzled stares from Pauline and others. "He's wearing a wonderful watch chain. He must be someone well off; certainly not a servant. He's dressed in Victorian garb like you."

The lady, conscious of being scrutinised, rejoins the group. Placated, the agitated man follows Pauline and the others from the room, glancing back a little uneasily towards the chair...still pulled out from the table.

SCHOLARLY PURSUITS?

The existence of this phantom scholar underlines the Library's function as a place of peaceful study. Unfortunately, this surface gloss hides a more disturbing aspect, as guide Patricia Davis attests.

Tricia explains: "When I first started here I didn't really think about the ghostly aspects until the night of another Ghost Evening. I was dressed as a 'rose lady' and had to do a quick change into a maid's outfit. When everyone had left the Library, and sure I wouldn't be disturbed, I undressed as quickly as possible. As I did, I became aware that I wasn't entirely alone, that someone was in there with me!

"The hairs on the back of my neck stood up. I can't explain the feeling. I hesitated, feeling so vulnerable."

Here again, the lighting had been purposely lowered to promote a supernatural mood, and left Tricia uncertain as to what the shadows really contained.

"It smelled like a match had been struck under my nose, the aroma of phosphorous filling the air. The smell really made my head go round. I thought - crikey, I hope there isn't a fire in here. I felt I should check, then told myself, No, there is someone in here and I don't like it. Still half undressed, I grabbed my clothes, dashed from the room and ran downstairs where I found Barbara Holton. 'Don't laugh at me, Barbara,' I blurted, 'but can I just tell you what's happened to me in the Library?'

"After hearing me out, Barbara said: 'Oh, don't worry about it, Trish, it's probably Little Sir John.'

"That distressed me. She was so matter-of-fact about it, she didn't laugh at me. And of course, at that time I didn't know anything about Little Sir John, I hadn't been here long enough.

"It was a menacing feeling, and is the only unpleasant thing I've experienced here. I felt that, I *definitely* felt that."

A picture materialises of an unseen watcher, nonchalantly observing, and appraising, a vivacious young woman, who remains oblivious to his presence until he betrays himself by lighting his favourite smoke.

But if not Victorian, could his earlier observer have been mistaken; might he have witnessed someone dressed in far older attire and failed to recognise it?

Barbara Holton could be correct in her assumption that the occupant is Little Sir John of the Great Beard, a man known to be dedicated to his books, and presumably not averse to the female form.

Whoever he was, on the first occasion he appears to be the victim, his solitude invaded by something from *our* present. On the second, and if he is the same individual, we see him taking advantage of an attractive young woman innocently revealing herself before him, and choosing to enhance the moment with his favourite tobacco, the heat from his match fracturing the fabric between two worlds.

"Time again, my Lord," echoes the voice. "It distorts." A pause before another more pertinent remark is made. "Perhaps you, Lord Byron, were the unseen observer."

Byron replies: "It is not unknown for me to succumb to such temptation." He smiles enigmatically, then continues, "Perhaps though you will recall that I have never found it necessary to conceal myself."

"Ah, I read your thoughts: you ask what is the mechanism that allows us such glimpses of parallel worlds. Do not forget, time and distance; light and distance - relative functions in life and death - are our medium here in Newstead.

"The force generated is energy often ignored. People exude their own aura, invisible to the naked eye, though it may be detectable should conditions dictate."

Byron is again aware of something watching him. He hears, "We are not simply memories, sir. Whatever, or whoever we are, we survive within the Library, are one with the Abbey, and others eventually become aware of us."

Who could own such a voice?

It is suspected that William Frederick Webb walks this house.

Ray Hadley is a tall man with silver hair, he wears gold-rimmed spectacles, and insists: "I tend to be cynical." However, his own less terrifying encounter is worthy of mention.

Ray is on the landing outside the Study, his authoritative air belying his approachability.

"I was sitting there." He indicates a plain wooden chair standing with its back to the stairs. He gazes across the deep red carpet and polished floorboards of the landing towards the Webbs' dressing-room. "It was around four o' clock one late September afternoon in 1993. It had been a dismal day, really grey and miserable outside, and lacking visitors."

Illumination from sombre wall lights and an old brass lamp on the wide oak table, sporting a green velvet cloth, lift a warm glow from the panelling and floors. Alongside Ray's chair stands the imposing grandfather clock, which started life in nearby Nottingham. It ticks quietly away, the only 'living' company on a slow day.

The trickle of visitors eventually ceases, but Ray cannot vacate his post until the Abbey finally closes its doors at 6 p.m. To relieve boredom, he proceeds to grapple with crossword clues. Behind him, the stairs wind down in three short flights to a dim lobby, each at right angles to the next, and separated by a small landing.

As Ray, pen in hand, concentrates on the clues, the stair-risers on the bottom flight creak upwards in almost casual succession. There then follows a brief pause after which the risers on the second flight follow suit.

"I thought little of it," Ray explains. "I didn't look around because I thought it was Graham, the Assistant Caretaker, on his rounds." He continues: "There came another brief pause, sufficient time for someone to cross the short landing between the flights. And then the top set of steps started to creak, again in succession up towards the one from the top."

Ray indicates the step in question. The chair still occupies that same position at the top of the stairs, only a foot away from that final step.

"I glanced over my shoulder expecting to see Graham, but he wasn't there, nor was anyone!"

A silence follows, giving time to absorb the significance of these words, this silence broken suddenly by the shrill chime of the massive clock at the quarter hour.

Ray looks down the stairs "...expecting to see someone fleeing after pulling the prank. I could see nothing, so I rushed down to the lobby, but the area was deserted. Had it been someone playing a trick, I would have seen them."

Descending the stairs, he says, "Let me show you something." Stopping at the last but one step, he presses firmly down on it with his foot. "This one creaks, so does one on the second flight, but only if you step on them in a certain way. Under the weight of only one person, no other step on these stairs makes any sound at all. They do, however, creak if two or more people use them at the same time."

But could the stairs be settling after their daily use?

Ray hesitates on his ascent to the second flight. "I've thought about that," he says, "but remember it had been a slack day. It must have been at least three quarters of an hour since they had last been used. Why should it take so long for them to start settling? And even if we accept it, why would they settle in sequence, one after another, from bottom to top, with just the right interval between each set of creaks?"

Gaining the landing, Ray glances back down the stairs. "This has been my only experience here. I'm not saying there couldn't be some explanation, but it would have to be a good one to convince me that something strange didn't happen that day."

If there is no physical explanation, then who could have ascended those stairs on that cheerless September afternoon? Or who would want to climb them in the direction of rooms previously occupied by William and Emilia Webb? Furthermore, who or what might be heavy enough to cause creaks which, under normal circumstances, only occurred under the weight of two or more persons?

William Frederick Webb, as indicated, was an imposing man of six foot four. Could some remnant of him, on occasion, journey to his study and dressing-rooms in that part of the house that he and his beloved Emilia had made their own? A house in which, by all accounts, they spent the happiest days of their lives?

Past and present merge, as happened when Maisie Hammond came into contact with the brown shape in the Becket Room.

III

Maisie Hammond's experience is evidence that not only do shades of the past exist alongside the living; living shades also form a part of the tapestry inside Newstead.

A wraith is the spiritual embodiment of a living person.

The Becket Room - said to owe its name to the tradition that Newstead Priory was founded in atonement for the murder of Thomas a' Becket in Canterbury Cathedral - is the destination to which Maisie heads this particular morning. "I'd been to Haidee Jackson's office, Haidee being the Chief Archivist at Newstead. I'd cleaned and had nothing on my mind at all."

The sunlight was limited, the shutters closed, Maisie making the point: "...you didn't get these particles of dust highlighted, nothing like that."

She pauses, an unscheduled break in her routine. "I felt as though I had actually walked through something, like a shaft of sunlight. My heart gave a sudden lurch. I can only liken it to the effect one gets when walking through an airport checkout and you're carrying your keys. It goes 'beep'. If I'd had palpitations, or anything wrong with me, the sensation would have continued, but I hadn't. I had this impression of a fairly tall, cream and brown shape.

"The sensation made me go all shuddery," Maisie states, "so I hurried upstairs feeling I needed to tell someone about it."

Maisie happens upon Enid, a cleaner, and reiterates her experience, wondering too, whether or not to mention it to Brian Ayers. She realises he would be busy at the reception desk and would not appreciate being disturbed.

Having unburdened herself to the cleaner, she puts the incident to the back of her mind and continues her duties. Her peace of mind is not to last. An hour later, around eleven o' clock, she returns to the kitchen where, to her surprise and consternation, she meets a lady named Georgina, who had worked at the Abbey some while ago. As Georgina turns towards her, an amazed Maisie notices that the visitor is attired in cream and brown!

Apparently, this friend had been touring the gardens in the company of one of the groundsmen, and had called in at the Abbey on impulse.

"It seemed strange that Georgina was standing there wearing the colours I felt I had walked through."

Precognition?

Maisie confirms: "I didn't know she'd been touring the gardens and just 'dropped in'. The first time I saw her she was in the kitchen about an hour after my experience."

"Perhaps confirmation of your own 'mirror image' being seen in two places at once, my Lord," the voice states. "Recall? You were observed in London whilst lying ill in Turkey!"

And what of the man in the Library? Another image transcending time instead of distance?

IV

As Newstead has grown, Byron agrees that, in a strange way, so has its strength. As a boy he was brought to Newstead to claim his inheritance - but *by whose choice?*

The Abbey and its domain *touched* him, motivated him to such a degree that later years would force him to write about the influences it fostered within him. In turn, these writings would broaden the world's knowledge; spread its story far and wide.

His fame and genius has helped to preserve Newstead. Until then it was a country house of little note and questionable architectural interest. Thus, in its own atypical way, the Abbey has ensured its continued survival, raising the disturbing concept that the building itself could be the main perpetrator in all the varied and often baffling occurrences.

Successors to the poet have felt the need to preserve the house, not only as a shrine to the 6th Lord but also because they have fallen prey to both its capricious attraction and unpredictable charm.

Newstead's fluctuating notoriety also dictates upon whom it will bestow its favours.

John Concannon, another guide here, is an iron-grey haired, down to earth individual with a dry sense of humour, and a mischievous sparkle in his eye. Comparable to a latter-day Joe Murray, John teases the visitor in not such ribald fashion about the Abbey's ghosts. Unlike his fellows, a disappointed John confesses to having had no similar experiences. Although a believer in the supernatural, he must content himself by resorting to his own witticisms. Alluding to sightings of a spectral hound roaming Newstead's corridors, John will glance behind the visitor, and comment: "That big dog's following you again." The bemused individual turns to find no dog present!

In his first week of working at the Abbey another guide experienced someone stroking his hair. Given the fact that he was ten miles away at the time, it naturally perturbed him so much so that he was constrained to say: "Whatever you are, please don't do that, it frightens me." His consternation prompted him to recite the Lord's Prayer, and fortunately, whatever it had been ceased to plague him further.

At a later date, a conversation between Christine Davies and a fellow guide was rudely interrupted.

Christine, a tall, elegant woman whose sometimes serious expression masks a wicked sense of humour, had this humour arrested when interrupted by what she terms 'a deep sigh.'

A link to the onset of heavy breathing heard by Jean Price in Byron's bedroom? Or the whispering of her own name heard by Tricia Davis?

Did the footsteps Nanny Smith heard proceeding from the coffin belong to the same presence that touched Barbara Holton? Perhaps those of the infamous Black Friar, once occupant of a coffin wrenched from beneath the Cloisters, torn open and subsequently despoiled, and deprived of long desired rest?

One night at home, Christine Davies is wrested from slumber by an invisible hand caressing her hair. Still half-asleep, and disbelieving, Christine asks, "Am I dreaming this?" Hoping the shadows hold no hidden terrors, her worst fears are realised. As she shakes off sleep the sensation persists. Feeling very alone, she appeals to her suitor to desist. Finally, after an interminable time, whatever had joined her heeds her pleas and abruptly departs.

"Past. Present. Future. All intertwined, Lord Byron. Perhaps now you begin to see that there is no end. I have cited several incidents of the Abbey's capacity and ability to reach out beyond its own walls and physical confines. Now hear this:

"We are brothers here, a community which cares for its own. Was that not our original intent? By being related, everything becomes relative. And must we not evangelise; spread our message far and wide?"

Therefore is the Abbey's power limitless, its reach totally unshackled, not least during Pauline Corby's aeroplane flight from San Francisco?

Was Pauline chosen to be its unconscious missionary? And might the American author, with whom she conversed, have been receptive to its hidden message; the delicate touch Pauline felt on her sleeve a response to some subtle contact?

Positive truth proves elusive, but their discussion regarding the Abbey most certainly triggered something. In turn this raises the disturbing possibility that both women did become involuntary channels through which it could extend its embrace.

Someone commented that for every good, there might well be an evil. Interestingly enough, this word, reversed, spells *live...*

So what else *lives* about this once religious house?

V

The voice says to Byron: "Now let us share a contemplative moment, as bread was shared in years passed."

"But where?" Byron enquires.

"Where else but the Refectory."

Set aside, yet still attached to the main building is a section, once used as servants' quarters, now adapted to and aptly named 'The White Lady Restaurant'.

In the days when Newstead was a priory, meals were communally taken in what was known as the 'Frater' or 'Refectory'. Here the 'Fraterer' would be responsible for its daily upkeep, his tasks including the checking of table-linen, crockery and eating implements. He would also check that the tables were laid correctly and that straw, scattered about the floor, was periodically changed.

This ritual now takes place in a more modern, streamlined location, the table manners of its patrons permitting wall-to-wall carpeting. Under the auspices of Ken Purslow and Maureen Crisp, today's pilgrims enjoy a menu that has given the restaurant its well-earned reputation.

Despite this, the 'White Lady' has its own share of unwelcome visitors!

Christine Marrison is bonny, approachable and not easily disturbed, her position as waitress in both Restaurant and in the downstairs Buttery, demanding virtually constant attendance.

"I've worked here since 1994, Christine states. "I've known it since Maureen, my sister-in-law, took it over. It's a weird sort of place, but nice really. None of us feel scared in the accepted sense.

"Sometimes, and I'm not sure if it's due to it being an old building or what, but I can be working on my own, peeling buckets of apples down here (The Buttery), and someone knocks on the counter. I turn to look and find there's no-one there. I did actually wonder if it has anything to do with the fridge mechanism. That said, it still sounds like somebody demanding attention. Sometimes, if you decide to take a breather, and sit at one of the tables to read your newspaper, you find it difficult to focus on the print because you're always obliged to inspect the room, to check if someone may have walked in. A peculiar feeling."

The Buttery walls are decorated with landscapes and personalities, some of which have Abbey connections; it is carpeted in green and gold, approximately forty feet long with mullioned windows and a semi-octagonal bar to the left of the counter. A welcoming room to which access is gained through a small lobby and stairs that lead to the first floor restaurant.

Apart from the Abbey kitchen in the South-West corner of the building, between the Hall and Refectory, the Buttery - according to Christine - formed a second kitchen because it boasts a dumb waiter.

THE WHITE LADY

Here, Christine sympathises with the Victorian
kitchen maids who refused to work alone in this
environment because they felt they were being watched.
"It leads you to believe there is somebody hanging
around. It's like the place is saying: 'You're not supposed
to have a break, we'll stop you whatever.'

So, the area not only boasts a dumb waiter, but a
silent observer!

Such observations are lent more substance by second
chef, Mark Milburn, an affable, twenty-something,
dark-haired and fresh-complexioned young man
employed at the White Lady since late 1996.

"Regularly," says Mark, "when I've been working in the Buttery's food preparation area, and before we open to the public, I've heard sounds coming from the main seating area, as though someone wants to gain attention by rapping on a table, or the counter, with their knuckles."

Both Christine and Mark are certainly unflappable individuals not given to flights of fancy, who both deny being scared. However, Christine will admit that she no longer desires to open up the restaurant if alone.

A telephone will ring for no apparent reason soon after their morning arrival. When either picks up the receiver, no-one answers. On yet another occasion, Christine placed a set of keys on the counter from where they disappeared never to be found!

Rapping. Telephone ringing. Keys disappearing. Is it then fair to speculate on whether this has something to do with Christine's sighting of a pale, female figure in the ground-floor preparation room, who stands where the work top now is; this work top evidently cutting through the image, which then fades?

"There is really no set pattern to it," she states. "Another peculiar incident occurred before we opened one evening. Linda Kershaw and Sandra Anderson, both part-time waitresses, were transporting bottles from the Cellar to the upstairs bar. Sandra had popped into the toilet whose door is adjacent to the Cellar door when suddenly the lights went off. Thinking what a stupid thing for someone to do, and put out by it, Sandra muttered irritably: 'Linda, why have you switched the lights off? I can't see a thing!' Perturbed that Linda was no longer around, Sandra hurried upstairs to challenge her. 'What are you playing at? Why have you switched off all the lights and banged the door?'

"Linda was pretty miffed by this, and retaliated with: 'I haven't been back down there!'

"Sandra remained convinced that someone had been outside the toilet, yet Linda remained adamant it wasn't her. This left Sandra scared out of her wits for the simple reason - as is the nature of Newstead - of there being no-one else around. Ever since the incident, they have refused to venture down there unaccompanied."

Each individual incident tends to parallel others, but none can be more disturbing than the strange shadow which has presented itself more than once on the first floor.

Mark Milburn declares: "Working in the Restaurant kitchen, we often leave the door open in order to see across the seating area and down the passage at the far end should anyone come in. Periodically, instinct forces you to look up. You see shadows. Seconds later, they've gone. Even when you investigate, I mean physically go and see, there's still nothing. That's what's really funny about it."

The Restaurant, like the Buttery, is a long, wide, well-lit room both day and evening, thus eliminating shadows. "But," Mark elaborates, "we do see shadows, and they move. Eerie when you consider there's nobody else here except us staff, and we're confined to the kitchen."

He goes on: "Sometimes we've been having a coffee break and the room grows very cold. It can be absolutely boiling when you sit after working hard, and especially if it's hot outside. But when you sit you're freezing."

It would naturally feel cooler inside on a hot day, yet Mark insists: "It's more than that, more like a cold spot."

Christine Marrison agrees. "This shadow is like someone coming into the restaurant, yet we know the doors are locked downstairs, so it's impossible. Like Mark says, you go to check and the room is empty.

"When you're not looking for it, it seems as if it's trying to attract attention. When you turn towards the stairs it moves away as though it's rushing to hide."

Christine and Mark conclude by saying respectively: "If I was scared I wouldn't come here. Nor would I dare open up in the morning."

Unfortunately, Mark Milburn's comment contradicts another, more disturbing incident.

"We were up in the restaurant one night, diners were finishing their meals, and I went up to the bar after we'd done. Glancing through the window, I saw this silhouette shaped like a cross, like someone with their arms stretched out. So I'm looking and thinking: What is it? But nobody wanted to go and check it out. Thinking safety in numbers, we all left together, relieved to notice the thing had gone.

"Next day I arrived to open the gate and something fell on me. It made me bloody jump. When I inspected it, it looked like a scarecrow, y'know like someone had made. It'd obviously been stuck in the middle of that stretch of grass, the big lawn before the West Front. Before I got here, somebody must have leaned it against the gate.

"It could have been kids messing about, but at night when it's dark and all you can see is this figure with arms akimbo, it puts you off. As soon as it fell on me I ran, thinking afterwards that Ken (Purslow) might have put it there, which he denied. Then again, there were campers in the area so I wouldn't have been surprised if it had been some of 'em messing about. Trouble is, when you don't know, it's best to leave well alone, especially in this place."

A joke? If so, is it human, or the supernatural playing its part? Another example of the Abbey's occupants exerting their influence?

Investigations lead to the conviction that this influence is used to attract, to detain, and ultimately to survive. There are those who have never left Newstead Abbey, equally there are others who have been summoned back.

CHAPTER NINE

VOICES

--oOo--

I

"You regale me with such tales," Byron says, eyes wide and wild, unable to truly believe what he hears. "We reside in this...this unrecognisable room with its counters, its tables and chairs...This eating place, and I hear tales of... of sightings...You tell me, what do they see?

"Damn you, are you real? If they might see you, then so should I. Who are you? TELL ME!"

But he doesn't wait for any revelation. Instead, he runs to the door, down the narrow stairs of the restaurant to follow the endless corridors, their stone reverberating with a trailing, chilling laugh.

Pausing, he listens, the laughter dying on a sigh, replaced now by a voice he knows. "Mother?" He glances around the corner to witness a female figure at her labours...

Maisie Hammond's early days here often resulted in feelings of isolation, even abandonment; more so when the house is closed to visitors.

Certainly others would be working only a short distance away, their presence easily forgotten.

Maisie worked with a will, duster in hand in the Charles II Dressing Room, the room devoid of furnishings, only the panelling and floors requiring attention.

"I was busy concentrating on what I was doing, when I felt conscious of being watched, that some*one*, or some *thing* lurked behind me. I hadn't heard anyone approach so I glanced up to check if the door to the boudoir was shut. It used to always be closed and it was on this day."

Even before she applied for the position, Maisie had heard of the Abbey's reputation. During those first weeks she was consoled to find that other staff had apparently adjusted to the unique atmosphere.

Desperate to become a member of 'the team', Maisie determined not to be panicked and tried to ignore any threatening vibes.

"I kept telling myself 'I'm all right'. I didn't talk to myself because I thought the others would think I was of a nervous disposition; that I didn't fit in. So you don't say these things for people to hear."

Who were these *others*? Those whom Maisie regarded as her supervisors, or those who remain hidden yet who *supervise* the *Supervisors*?

"I was determined to stick it out," says Maisie, "and I did. But nothing would induce me to look over my shoulder."

Byron reaches out in vain; very aware that the woman he sees remains untouchable. His mind races, the object of his initial pursuit no longer there.

His hands fly to his head in attempt to wrest the pain of thinking. "Am I being driven mad, beyond all hope of redemption? What is the purpose, if all are related, all is relative, why then are we denied relationships?"

Time, as usual, distorts. Byron flung forward to confront a figure, laden by woe, easily identified as a reflection of his own distress...

It is a Saturday morning. Susan Patching is opening up the room next door to the Charles II Room.

"I'd had a bad morning at home," Susan says, " and felt a bit down when I arrived for work. As I opened the blinds in the Dressing Room, I let out this huge, sorrowful sigh. A few seconds later there was another sigh behind me. I turned round thinking it was Geoff, another guide, coming to help me, and he'd heard me sigh. We do play tricks on each other, and I thought he was taking the mickey. To my consternation the room was empty. I wouldn't say I was scared, but feeling below par made me really alarmed."

The 'presence' was alive too, and apparently concerned about Sue's feelings!

Byron turns away, thinking: If I cannot be, how then can I feel? "Does this place *attract* and ultimately *select* those who care for it? Do I have a say in such matters? And might they sense me? Is it that they are allowed some privilege of seeing and experiencing its mysteries?"

The people who work at Newstead readily accept that they are not alone in looking after this great house with its many historic connections, and that some of its former inhabitants will have their say.

The word 'some' is used advisedly since the question has not been resolved as to whether or not there is more than one presence here.

Byron stands in the Great Hall, mind reeling from these revelations. He finds himself again confronted by a woman dressed in clothes similar to those he has already seen.

Tricia Davis: "When I opened the curtains in the Great Hall a couple of years ago, it was almost as if someone stood behind me. It's just that feeling, one not easily explained to anyone. It's very odd."

Individuals hear voices in Byron's rooms, and in the Charles II Room, and something did accompany Brian Ayers onto the roof the day he met with his accident. The feeling of being watched is absolute between Newstead's guides and is sometimes accompanied by a knowledge of being protected.

Does a single presence roam the House? Or a selection of multiple presences, some tied to a particular location, others free to move at will?

Voices emanate from walls, from panelling:
'George...you are not alone.'

"Scrope Davies?" Byron turns, eyes searching, seeing nothing.

'My son...talk with me...'

"Mother? Dearest mother...where? I smell your perfume..."

The scent of roses lures him down ill-lit corridors, in and out of rooms, a dimly lit shade always just ahead.

He is stopped short by another recognisable tone, this time deeper, manly. *'Another draft, Abbot?'*

"Be damned, it is Matthews." He whirls, a shadow darts away. "Wait. Don't go."

Lucy calls: *'Come, my lord, I am lonely for your embrace. Tell me you love me.'*

He glances up the winding stair, each step taken slowly, mind desperately attempting to understand just how it is possible to hear voices from *his* past.

And all the while, hidden deep within those friendly utterances, is something dark, containing a fearful intimation.

Dare he proceed?

"George. George, will you not join me? How can it be wrong to...love?"

His hand rests on the door handle. "Augusta?" Her name on his lips, he opens the door...

Onto night...a feeling of suffocation...

A glimpse of his old dressing room -

The Prior's Oratory.

II

The Prior's Oratory, a cold, inhospitable room, is the black heart of the Abbey, made positive by a chain of happenings experienced by staff and visitors alike.

Once a place of pain - from the Abbey's inception to its dissolution - and a place where the canons' associations and lives would terminate. Some would yield calmly to the call of their Maker, for others the passage would be torment, these sad souls reproaching themselves for past indiscretions, yet most anticipating a reward of long, peaceful slumber.

Not to be!

Disinterred coffins! The long sleep of the dead disturbed!

Fact!

Good and evil, like love and hate, represent two sides of the same coin. Tossed at the peril of those seeking guidance, the coin, once flipped, prevents our knowing upon which side it will fall.

On a rare occasion a coin will land on its edge, balanced in some unnoticed, hidden crevice in the woodwork...So, which way then? And, more important...indeed more disturbing, which way do *others* go?

Do we dare follow the darker track of the dead?

Dare Lord Byron follow this same track?

THE BLACK HEART OF THE ABBEY

III

"We are in the Prior's Oratory..."

Maisie Hammond, out of all who work at Newstead, is perhaps the one most susceptible to its influence, not least its more disturbing aspects.

A group of thirty and more people on a guided tour stand enthralled by her narrative.

"The Prior's Oratory is the most haunted room in the Abbey..." She relates how it used to be the last resting place of the canons...And pauses, sounds and voices diminish. Her speech falters, she blurts out: "Ooh, there's something happening to me. And it's not because you're visitors... No... No, I'm not acting, it's not because you're visitors." She stammers a little; then recovers. "I'm sorry ladies and gentlemen but you will have to leave now." At this, Maisie opens the door and shepherds them to the top of the stairs.

Returning to the room she attempts, in seclusion, to come to terms with what has happened.

Thankfully, the room has regained its innocence. Calmer, Maisie attempts to reconcile what seized her both from within and without.

"As I was talking to the party, it was as though a cloak - I call it a cloak...I don't know...a garment...like a cloak was thrown across my shoulders. I placed my hands across my chest in an effort to take the weight because I found it to be so heavy I felt I should be bending at the knees.

"There is more. There was something actually coming up through my body and holding me upright. Had I wanted to bend, I was prevented from doing so by this...this force.

"I was standing sort of, oh, my normal stance when addressing people. It was just this *feeling* that actually came through me. Like electricity, a tingling feeling giving me the energy to make me believe I was a taller person. Later, I spoke to another staff member apparently similarly affected. She told me: 'You were taking on the form of a taller person'. Yet, even she could not fully explain what it was I had experienced.

"Despite other experiences, this is the one which I found most disturbing at the time. It was just this not knowing what was happening to me because, as I say, I kept wrapping my hands about me due to the pressure on my shoulders. Yes, this will actually stay with me all the time."

Nor does this disturbing episode terminate here.

"We had this gentleman named John Watts," Maisie says, "a Shakespearean actor who, during our tours, would appear at a given time as Lord Byron, dressed in period costume and reading to himself. On one occasion I showed him the Oratory and explained I would be acting the part of housekeeper during the tour and would bring visitors up here to relate this little ghost story.

"This prompted me to reiterate my earlier experience in response to which he actually flung his cloak across my shoulders. It was so heavy, almost suffocating and it scared me. I pleaded: 'Take it off me, please. Take it off me!' The tingling sensation returned and I relived what had happened before. It was the feel and weight of the cloak that did it!"

Encounters of this type do not respect the individual, this specific incident a reminder of Brian Ayers 'cloak of ice' from which, for hours, he could not be rid.

Another guide, Audrey, went through a similar experience in the Oratory. And Barbara Holton found herself gasping for breath in the same room.

Maisie explains: "Barbara is not asthmatic, but she couldn't breathe, there was a pressure on her chest. We have a number of visitors who get the same sensation when they come in here as if there isn't any air. Many visitors will not even come past the door."

Sue Patching also confirms: "I think most of us have experienced this 'swimmy thing'. The Oratory is a really weird room."

And maybe it is its own master because, as Sue again relates: "When I was up in the Oratory I've had other strange sensations, not least on the day the door leading from Byron's bedroom into the Oratory wouldn't open." Frustrated by this, and anxious about her duties, she hissed, "Come on, for goodness sake, I'm in a hurry." The next minute it opened.

Do we know what opened it?

IV

These incidents are far from being the full extent of sensations experienced in this same room.

Towards the close of a season, Wendy, a co-worker, said to Maisie Hammond, "Ooh, that room's ever so strange up there, the one with no furniture. The sensation I got was as though I was being 'twirled around'."

This reminded Maisie of another episode involving a smaller party of four or five people. This time, not forgetting her earlier experience, she had decided not to offer too much detail concerning the haunted room. She had also concluded that she would "... just mention it very quickly and they'll go.

"I decided to tell them the story about the cloak and straightaway felt giddy. I actually asked a lady guest: 'Now am I standing still, or am I rotating?'"

Somewhat puzzled, she replied, "You're perfectly still."

Maisie went on to elaborate. "Well, the sensation I'm getting through the middle of this floor is as though I were being rotated. When I explained this to Wendy, she told me, 'I felt exactly the same thing'.

"When I walk through the door leading from Byron's bedroom across the Oratory to its adjacent door, you'd think my legs had actually turned to lead. Considering I've come running up the stairs and gone about my duties cleaning the room, checking it, I am disturbed to realise that as soon as I reach the middle of the floor I feel as though I'm encased in lead."

She glances uneasily around the Oratory searching for words. "I get the same dragging feeling that you get when you're ill. It's as if I've been taken over...yes, possessed by somebody who isn't very well, and who isn't able to walk properly either."

The implication here is obvious, but Maisie remains unconvinced. When asked to agree it may be something to do with the poet, she observes: "Then again, we're going way, way back in history, possibly even further than Byron."

A connection to the Black Friar?

Maisie Hammond does not answer directly but eventually reiterates the visit of the Leicestershire medium, brought to Newstead Abbey for the programme 'Ghosts in Stately Homes'.

We should recall that Byron had a page in attendance who would have slept in that room. Furthermore, a small, fair-haired child (boy?) has been observed here.

And another visitor, according to Maisie, a small man and born-again Christian, reacted so violently to its atmosphere that he ran around the room crying: "No ghost here - evil from within 'other people'."

Another question?

An observant visitor to the Prior's Oratory will doubtless notice at the very centre of the floor a shape strongly resembling an embryo - a sign perhaps that we are in the very womb of the house from whence all things are sent forth?

If so, why? An inevitable conclusion is that some unfortunate child suffered unimaginable and subsequently fatal punishment, even a gross act of indecency within these walls, many years before.

It is perfectly possible that the anguish suffered by the child may have so charged the room, turning it into an engine sometimes generating uncontrollable forces. Or has fashioned the room into the vehicle by which forces already present are concentrated prior to their re-distribution.

It is hardly surprising then, since Byron adopted this as his dressing room, that some vestige of the poet does remain.

Pain in the temples, nausea, and many similar occurrences imply a highly charged atmosphere akin to that surrounding high voltage equipment. But, unlike the medium, for some the source remains just beyond their reach. Maisie Hammond and others struggle to explain the sensation.

"The feeling is projected outwards. You expect to see..." She hesitates.

The Abbey's foundation is built on religion, which adds to this already potent mixture, overtones of which we have already witnessed.

Neither must we ignore a totally unscripted remark Maisie Hammond made to a group of female visitors: "I will have to go to a spiritualist meeting shortly, hopefully to clear my mind of this experience."

Obviously, what she had undergone had affected Maisie more deeply than she cared to admit, prompting her to seek some form of absolution.

Finally, an incident involving another woman who, staggering from the room, told Maisie: "I felt I was swimming." So affected was she that she gave Maisie a small, wooden cross insisting she wear it henceforth.

As is well known, this Christian object is used regularly to ward off evil.

V

Power and force.

In considering the source of the power of Newstead we should analyse the word *supernatural* - beyond nature. 'Nature' is what we know, or perhaps *think* we know. No scientific explanation is offered here, but it seems that all matter is nothing more, at the most minute level, than particles of energy locked into the forms we recognise by forces impossible to imagine.

Matter is no more than a small disturbance on an ocean of energy, everything around us, ourselves included, as insubstantial as dreams. Such concepts take us beyond nature and its commonly understood logic.

Light and sound are energy from specific, and often, natural sources, so why, we ask, should an environment such as Newstead not generate, and possibly concentrate energy? It varies in both pattern and intensity, often hardly noticeable, but on many occasions becomes so intense as to interfere with the house's own installations.

Strangely, its alarms are triggered without benefit from human contact. More notably its light-switches become capable of offering 'an unexpected shock'?

Bryan Ayers' birthday at the end of July was the usual enjoyable event, all those present celebrating with enthusiasm. On the following morning, a Sunday, Maisie Hammond undertook her usual rounds only to discover all the lights had been left burning. She silently chastised the person she deemed responsible, muttering to herself: "Ray, you've left all the lights on."

Thinking to rectify the situation, she groped for a switch and instantly felt her hand gripped. Startled, she turned expecting to see one of Bryan's guests. There was no-one. She states: "The hand felt clammy, as though the person had just bathed. Indeed I returned several times to check if there was anything that might explain the cause.

"I did in fact turn off the lights, but found them on again the next morning."

It is worth noting that Byron used the Slype, off the Cloisters, as a bathing pool!

Energy. And source.

Little is known of the land before it was claimed by the Church. It is unlikely that such a favoured place would have remained unoccupied until then, but the use to which it was put in those pre-Christian times remains a mystery; marks of its habitation dating back through the Dark Ages to pre-history having been obliterated by subsequent developments.

In relation to this, the answer could be even more fundamental, and discovered in the very structure, or location of the land itself. Manifestations, as we have seen, are not confined to the Abbey buildings. Might there be some distinct characteristic that endows the site with a singular energy, focussed by the hideous history of the building's bleak centre - the Prior's Oratory?

The phrase *supernatural force* warrants further scrutiny.

To make a further, more emboldened supposition, and given the fact the Oratory is the hub of so many inexplicable happenings, could the Black Friar be its chilling emissary?

He has never appeared in the Oratory but is perhaps a manifestation of the forces expelled by it. Whether malignant, or benign, whether light or sound, or any form of energy travelling from its source, it is obviously apparent only when detected. So, is the Friar the 'embodiment' of whatever issues from that room, perhaps even the instigator of every episode involving his living counterpart - whether chosen, or who accidentally cross his path?

And one of these 'embodiments' is, of course, his own.

Both a challenge to, and an explanation of, the possible process is offered by quantum physics in a concept which the untutored mind finds almost impossible to comprehend. The tiny, sub-atomic particles of which everything is constructed do not actually travel from place to place, instead they appear and disappear spontaneously in each location, as do apparitions. Further, they communicate without contact, acting on each other even at a distance. This same process is responsible for concepts such as extra-sensory perception that does not require the transmission of any message or energy from one being to another. This energy is all around us, latent in the Universe waiting to be composed into the image which forms directly in the brain by-passing the sensory organs.

It follows, that no source or hidden transmitter is required; whatever creates these illusions does so using these, as yet, ill-understood mechanisms.

Maisie Hammond explains in her quiet, dignified way, that during the course of her duties, she was dusting and polishing the office of the Chief Archivist, Haidee Jackson.

Involved in her task, and glad of the quiet, Maisie heard the sound of footsteps climbing the stone stairs leading to the landing directly outside the office. "Haidee always wears black clothes and has black hair," Maisie explains. "It was about the time she was due to come to the office so I thought little of it. Picture me, only five foot tall, cleaning behind the high desk and thinking, if I don't get up from behind here I'll frighten her. Obviously she couldn't know I was there as I'd closed the door behind me.

"I rose slowly to avoid that dizziness one gets when rising too quickly - sometimes you get things swimming before your eyes when you do that. I waited for her to come in."

A quiet office, a little off the normal thoroughfare for staff, it encapsulates the lulling effect of the Abbey. Here is Maisie waiting to welcome a colleague, the door is closed, the room a turgid grey, so reminiscent of the month of February.

"There was no sunlight to cast shadows in the room from trees or anything. I waited for the door to open, but it didn't. I knew I'd heard those little steps coming up the stairs, so I thought perhaps Haidee was carrying something and struggling with the door.

"Recollect, there were no shadows whatsoever, but suddenly there was this black..." Definitive words, conclusive of the power of Maisie's conviction. "It came from the door, and crossed to the window. And no, it wasn't Haidee!

"I glanced towards the door to check if it was open. It wasn't. I could feel my heart racing. I didn't want to look back towards the window but felt compelled to. I can't tell you the relief I felt when I saw the shape, the thing, whatever it was, had vanished."

Does she know what she saw?

Indisputably, Maisie does feel that on that grey, February day she saw the Black Friar.

So did it choose to make its presence known to her, or was it engaged in some timeless, repetitive ritual?

Did some mechanism akin to the wheels of a clock operate, such devices following some pre-ordained pattern, moving endlessly to a soft, insistent rhythm? And as these forms, these forces, trace their given path around the Abbey, they leave behind their own, individual signature - the smell of roses, a sudden chill, the sound of footsteps.

Yet, as soon as we convince ourselves that it is all entirely impersonal, we are driven back by more profound evidence which prompts the question: Could at least some of the forces at work here have an even more sinister motivation?

Is it *'the dead, but sceptered sovereigns, who still rule our spirits from their urns?'*

For this evidence we should return to events surrounding Newstead during the English Civil Wars.

VI

These examples may, or may not be connected, but are without doubt, bound to the same place. Why should a Cavalier be 'tied' to the Webbs' room? Is it one of the Byron brothers, possibly one of the four who did not survive the Civil War? Or it may be Sir John Byron himself, this unfortunate, labelled 'a dangerous delinquent' who died in exile in Holland. Of course, it could well be a less noteworthy victim of the siege who died defending the Abbey, one whose passing has not been logged in history's books.

Throughout the Civil War it is documented that meetings were held, tactics discussed and plots hatched at Newstead. As late as 1648, Colonel Gilbert Byron and Lord Richard Byron were working to revive royalism locally in preparation for the Second Civil War - in early June of that year they attempted to take Nottingham by force, the attack eventually beaten off. This resulted in many casualties, and many taken prisoner, some of the casualties possibly brought back to Newstead to die within its walls.

The Byron family were fined for their part in the Civil Wars, and for some years Newstead was managed by sequestration commissioners to meet the fines.

Bloodshed and blood stains these dismal times, its signs permanently etched - yet another mirror throwing back semi-permanent reflections.

VII

All of the staff at Newstead have, in their own way, come to terms with their experiences. But for some such as Margot Miller, Patricia Davis and Jean Price who glimpsed another less innocuous face, the event is forever with them. Amongst them is Barbara Holton...

In September 1995, at six-thirty on another of Newstead's Ghost Evenings, Barbara was being driven to the Abbey by her husband to take part in the proceedings as guide and role player, eventually to dress as a Victorian chamber maid.

Night had fallen as they approached, darkness intensified by a lack of lighting along the narrow drive; Newstead's lighted windows offering some comfort in this oppressive gloom. Stopping the car before the front entrance, both noticed a robed figure through the building's bowed windows, climbing the South Stairs.

"John's eager tonight," Barbara's husband commented, referring to John Concannon who assumes the role of the Black Friar on these occasions.

Barbara laughed as they climbed from the car and entered the Abbey. "I've just seen John going up the stairs," she said to a gathered group of colleagues. "He's anxious to get started."

"John?" they quizzed in unison.

"Yes. John Concannon going up the South Stairs, and changed already," Barbara reiterated.

"But John hasn't arrived yet," someone replied. And, as though on cue, John Concannon, the counterfeit monk, joined them as they spoke, attired in suit and overcoat.

"Then who-?" Quizzed Barbara, answering her own question by adding, "it's probably Brian, he wears dark things."

It seems Brian Ayers was around, and going about his business checking equipment in some other part of the building!

Brian's role on such evenings is to skip unseen about the building managing sound and lighting effects.

Time passed; everyone now changed into 'role playing attire' and taking up their respective positions throughout the Abbey. Guests arrived and after a welcoming glass of wine, the tour got underway.

Brian Ayers made his way to the Minstrel's Gallery overlooking the Great Hall, preparing to operate necessary equipment. Most of the lights throughout the path of the tour had been extinguished leaving only muted illumination to enhance the atmosphere. Brian carried a torch to light his own way. As he moved towards the Gallery stairs, a tall, black shadow filled the beam, vanishing as quickly as it had appeared. Guests could be heard climbing the stairs behind him, necessitating his urgent attendance on the Gallery above, so depriving him of time to reflect on, or become alarmed by, the event.

Around nine thirty, Barbara Holton and Susan Patching, chatted together in the Library as they waited their turn in the play.

Hearing the group enter the Great Hall, off the West Gallery, Sue left Barbara and walked along the East Gallery to take up her own position. In doing so, she became involved in a puzzling episode.

"As I was going along," she says, "I felt as though I'd passed through something very cold, as if there were a door or window open. That's how it felt. I sort of turned, went back to check, but discovered nothing. Presumably, whatever had caused it had moved on, the Gallery air as still and dead as always. Later, when I mentioned it to someone, that person said, 'Oh, it's not the first time. These things happen.'

"I've since learned," Sue comments, "that other people have been similarly affected. But, on that night that chill through which I passed seemed to be moving towards the Library."

'A strange cold thaw upon the heart.'

Alone, Barbara waited in the Library. "All the curtains and blinds were drawn apart from the one blind next to the Library door. I stood by this window; the light off in the room. I was about to go to the far door to check if the visitors were coming so that I knew when I would be doing my thing. I didn't bother to put on the light.

"The dimensions of the Library make it difficult to negotiate especially with the numbers you get on such evenings. To avoid accidents, we move the furniture from the centre of the room."

This serves a twofold purpose, the second being to allow Barbara to walk without encumbrance. "I had a good walk round and knew I wouldn't fall over anything," she observes.

"I stood by this window in order to grow accustomed to the gloom. As I gradually did, something strange started happening, a weird, grey light filled the room; I was able to pick things out quite clearly. It wasn't just that my eyes were becoming accustomed to the dark; no, there was light in the room. There was a greyness around me, and I could see that the door at the opposite end, open when I came in, had closed. Curious, I started to walk towards it, but when I reached about halfway, this form rose from the floor. I was more or less at the room's centre, over to the left by the settee. I stopped, no longer curious, simply petrified. By this time I was about two feet away from it.

"It was very black, and grew taller and taller until it towered above me. I couldn't move, just simply stood there and watched it rise!"

Barbara raises a hand above her head to indicate how tall she considered the shape to be. Barbara is approximately five foot in height. "...At least six foot," according to her, "...and it came to a slight point."

Still glued to the spot, and perhaps beyond fear, one thought alone commandeered her: What the devil is this? What is it?

"I couldn't do much else," she says. "I've never been so terrified. I kept hoping it was someone playing a trick, and remember wondering whether that was it. But straightaway I knew it wasn't, nobody could make a thing rise out of nowhere like that did. It was so scary.

Even then I still kept wondering what I was seeing. There was no face at all, just a shape, a solid, black shape with a very slight point at the top of the figure."

Barbara gathers her thoughts, clearly ill at ease with her memories. "I froze, but of course my mind was still going, and I was thinking: What is it? WHAT IS IT? The hairs on my neck just went up.

"I knew it wasn't a human-being coming up, as it seemed to, through the floor."

Regaining some composure after reliving the experience, Barbara feels able to continue: "The room didn't feel cold, and I didn't feel cold, but my heart was thumping nineteen to the dozen. I was frightened...it really did scare me. I didn't stop to see it disappear, I just turned and ran from the room and kept on running until I reached the Manuscript Room where I discovered the next 'real' person. Only then did I stop running, exhausted but grateful of the respite. It really did me and I still, to this day, don't really know what it was I saw.

"I did come back later when the lights were properly on, but there was nothing." She offers a relieved smile and jokes, "I certainly wouldn't have come back when the lights were off; not that night anyway."

Is it possible she might have been affected by the atmosphere created on a Ghost Tour evening?

Barbara remains adamant: "I don't know. I know what I saw, and I know what I felt."

A visitor strayed from the main party then?

"I've thought about that," she states seriously, "but I doubt it because this materialised through the floor in front of me. It rose but remained within the floor. It didn't hover.

"I watched it grow, following it up like this with my head and eyes. I didn't know how far it was going you see. It was most unnerving." Her laugh is a nervous outburst, a relieving of tension. "More than that, it frightened me. I'm no heroine, I'm a coward and don't mind admitting it when it comes to things like that. 'He who fights and runs away, lives to fight another day!'

"I've often wondered what I would do if I did see something. Now I know...I'd run away."

Barbara Holton adopts a thoughtful expression and says: "It's the first thing I've 'seen' in all my years here...and it really unnerved me."

Those familiar with Byron's verse will recognise the shape that confronted Barbara Holton that night:

'His form you may trace, and not his face,
'Tis shadowed by his cowl;
But his eyes may be seen from the folds between,
And they seem of a parted soul.'

This once again poses the question: Could the poet have actually seen the Black Friar?

VIII

Why did Newstead wait three decades before it chose its emissary to confront Barbara Holton? She might not have been singled out; she could merely have been yet another innocent caught in the wrong place at the wrong time, and fallen foul of Newstead's complicated mechanisms.

Geographically, the South Stairs lead us from a

lobby just off the Crypt, taking us to the first floor and the doors into the Great Hall. Within the Crypt lies a stone coffin, that same sarcophagus which was being dusted by Barbara Holton when she felt the touch of a hand upon her head. And perhaps similar to that very same coffin which, according to Nanny Smith, reposed outside the Great Hall during the 6th Lord's time at Newstead, and from which his own servants ran terrified.

Nanny Smith blamed that particular coffin for the footsteps, and the locked door she experienced one night. This is echoed years later when Susan Patching was unable to open the door to the Prior's Oratory.

There is but one possible conclusion. Something is drawn from this coffin to wander the halls and corridors. Perhaps there is, amongst Newstead's assorted manifestations, one main protagonist who makes his mostly covert rounds, but who, on occasion, is drawn to make his presence known. Sometimes his demeanour is munificent, sometimes playful, but on other occasions, intimidating. Why, remains a mystery.

There is no set pattern, or if there is, it remains blurred.

Ray Hadley explains: "Instances of haunting appear to come in batches." In saying this, it could mean that when a particularly vivid example occurs, a victim's compulsion to unburden himself to others, brings to mind less remarkable instances which might hitherto go unnoticed.

Newstead's personnel have ceased to regard as noteworthy such actions as the feel of a hand brushed through hair; the touch of fingers on a face; of being observed; of occasional aromas. It is only when prompted, they will talk about them.

Interestingly, should these happenings be properly and scientifically logged over a specific period, they might yet be matched to some confluence of physical events. We already accept the Moon as being the over-riding reason for spring's exceptional tides.

If we adopt the comforting, less controversial position that these phenomena are some innocent vestige, without will, an event occurs which rebuts such innocent assumptions.

Six months after her ordeal, Barbara reiterated her experience to Pauline Corby in the very room wherein it occurred, only this time in daylight.

Newstead had yet to open its doors that day, so the two ladies were enjoying the lull. In the solitude, noise deadened by drapes and rich carpeting, Pauline casually leaned with her leg into one of the heavy Library tables and listened to Barbara as she described the black shape that had risen up before her. Without warning the table suddenly *moved.*

Pauline explains: "It literally lifted and moved position, as if something had picked it up and set it down again. It exposed the indentations in the carpet which marked its former position." She places her hand under the table's edge and challenges, "Try lifting it."

The table is surprisingly heavy, no one person of ordinary strength able to lift it. But perhaps Pauline's own weight pressed against it had caused the movement? Considering Pauline can only be of average weight, and much less than that required to re-locate such an object, this explanation is doubtful.

"Anyway," Pauline interjects, "I was leaning against it. SO WHY DID IT MOVE TOWARDS ME? That table jumped! It really did ...jump! It almost levitated, that type of thing.

"I was really concentrating hard on what Barbara was telling me, then the table moved. Barbara said to me, 'What the hell are you doing?'

"I suppose," Pauline continues thoughtfully, "it could have been the weight of the table striking the floor, but I swear I felt the whole room shudder, like an earth tremor."

This post-script to Barbara Holton's terrifying evening further demonstrates that something *is* watching, and *is* aware of human presence at Newstead. And can, if it so wishes, react for good or bad.

According to legend, the Black Friar appears as a harbinger of dark tidings. In 1995, unknown to Abbey staff, proposals to undermine Newstead from nearby Annesley Colliery were being considered, the resulting damage likely to render the Abbey structurally unsafe causing its permanent closure and subsequent demise.

Did the presence of the Black Friar presage certain events? A subsequent public outcry was swiftly followed by the closure of Annesley Colliery thus preserving the Abbey, possibly, and hopefully, in perpetuity. Good and evil do co-exist here, marked by the telling smells of flowers and sulphur, just two things that underline this fact, thereafter proving Newstead's remarkable potential for self-preservation.

Has the Black Friar's appearance prevented another re-formation?

But there may be a significance greater than any so far considered, one supported by the natural agencies already explored. Pauline experienced 'an earth tremor' - energy released deep underground, elemental forces beyond control.

Energy nurtured within, then collected from the soil upon which Newstead Abbey has been created, to be reconstituted in whatever form - good or evil - within the Prior's Oratory. If true, then perhaps man should think twice before disrupting such ground, meddling with the unfathomable!

It is not simply a passive force, nor is it confined to Newstead's immediate vicinity; history dictating what misfortunes befell the last occupants who were guilty of such desecration.

The sheer volume, variety and persistence of events described lead to one conclusion: That at Newstead the natural and supernatural have become fused in a unique fashion possibly accelerated by the poet Byron himself...

CHAPTER TEN

BARE BONES

--oOo--

I

An icy draught permeates the Oratory, Byron suddenly fighting for breath.

He supports himself on the wall suddenly very aware of his glimpse of the future, of the woman who felt dizzy and yet remained upright. Determined he will not fall, he tries to remember if the room had been lit when he entered.

Had it been so, then it isn't any longer; vapid darkness impregnating every corner; overlaying every wall; the window an even blacker maw.

He gropes at the walls, frantically searching for a door, his attention diverted by a soft whimper issuing from a far corner. He challenges. "Who's there? Who are you that you disrupt me so? And why are you so distressed?"

Silence, oppressive yet infinitely preferable to the soft, taunting song which followed, hummed softly by a voice barely recognisable

"I know you, so why do you not acknowledge me?" Names reverberate. "Caroline? Edleston?" Edleston!

That fixation, that pretty boy friend from the poet's formative years, merely another love in an endless, frustrating quest.

"Damn you, Edleston, why did you die at such an early age? I idealised you, perhaps wrongly, but then how am I to tell...? Time *is* my enemy."

He whimpers like the thing in the shadows distressed by tumbling images.

Could the vocalist be Nicolo Giraud, that other boy, his companion in Greece, sixteen years old and dedicated to his mentor?

Byron's hand scratches the stonework, a futile gesture, symbolically erasing the past and diverting him from thoughts of the future. He yells again, "Who are you? Identify yourself. And be warned, I carry loaded pistols!"

The room encompasses a strange, somehow unearthly silence once more, this sullen quiet rendered by a scream so dreadful the atmosphere becomes cauterised. A resulting pulse of light reveals the writhing form of a woman at his feet.

His eyes grow wide, this apparition so...so recognisable. "Ada." He feels even more distraught, and wonders what vile entity has sought to direct his wretched thoughts to things he would rather not know. "Ada, it is you?"

Eyes meet, one pair shocked, the other demanding, a plea in them. He feels her agony, and his hand closes about the butt of a pistol projecting from his waistcoat pocket. He baulks at the task, thinking: Not even for you, even as another profound thought inveigles itself: How then can I kill the already dead?

"Why me?" He demands to know, any answer lost as the room is reinvested with sound, voices raised in dispute, and in laughter - songs from one corner; sounds of familiar carousing, and here the soft pleas of a woman; there, a sudden clatter as something strikes the wall, causing him to duck.

As suddenly, curses impregnate, vile, taunting, they betray their owner's identity.

"Oh God, Mother...Do you still not rest? Does your inveterate anger still go unappeased?"

No sooner one, than something more, rushes to take its place...to tantalise. Hot, male breath on his face, a whispered suggestion.

Byron hurriedly backs away. "De Ruthyn, you animal, leave me. GO!"

"George. George." Another female voice courts him.

"Mary?" Byron responds. "But which Mary?"

No answer, simply tinkling laughter, fading. All subside, the room taking on a different atmosphere, lit now by a curious glow. Cold mist hangs like Arctic fog. And there is the far door. He moves towards it brought to an abrupt halt by something slowly issuing from that irregular, embryonic shape at the floor's centre, the shape even now glowing with pale luminosity.

A familiar, frightening shape, glimpsed before, so long ago, seen in the future too. First the cowl, hiding the visage beneath, the one he has never seen. Broadish shoulders top a bulky frame, and even as Byron desires to know, the face remains coated by oval shadows.

'I see a dusk and awful figure rise,
Like an infernal god, from out the earth;
His face wrapt in a mantle, and his form
Robed as with angry clouds...'

"YOU!" Byron sounds resigned, obliged to accept this ordained meeting. "An encounter too long overdue, my pleasure now somewhat muted by my circumstances."

"And what circumstances are they, pray?"

Byron appraises what is before him without question. But the voice carries none of the room's reverberations, the tone lacking any real substance, is more like an echo in his own mind - thoughts voiced in the form and shape of another. And perhaps promoted by the very fabric of Newstead itself.

Byron offers a sardonic smile, thinking to go along with this unusual play. "Circumstances," he repeats the word. "I should have no need of explanation, especially to you."

"Why especially to me?" The voice resonates. "Do we not share a common situation, you and I, perhaps only differing in our lineage?"

"Lineage?"

"Indeed, for what we have in common is this house, though where we differ is by virtue of the fact that you choose to remain, whereas I am brought back against my will."

"From this then, my lord, you must also ask of us both: Who am I?"

Byron nods curtly, runs a hand through dark curls. "We must therefore introduce ourselves. You, I presume, are one of those whom my illustrious ancestors so cruelly dispossessed, and I... I... " He hesitates, searching his person, patting his 'substance'. "I am...?" He concludes there is no real answer, and the echo lingers: "Who. Or. What. Am. I?"

"Sir, you presume too much. You recognise a shape, thus believing you recognise *me*. It is true the Canons of Saint Augustine held this place and did not willingly relinquish their hold. They never have, for evidence of ownership is never far away. I charge that you think of others, some of your blood line, others with whom you cannot be acquainted, and one with whom you are, without doubt, most intimately acquainted."

Byron frowns, he is puzzled by this, any answer evasive.

Conscious of a beckoning hand, he follows the gliding shape into the adjoining bedroom, the other's words trailing. "Come, my lord," it says, "you may ask where does it all begin, and I suggest that this site's very history holds the answers."

In the bedchamber the poet takes his favourite seat. He gazes through the window across the broad, placid lake. Behind him, the figure remains at the threshold. Slowly, it begins to relate Newstead's history from its earliest times. It offers a tantalising insight into the Abbey's peculiar, and enigmatic character...

II

The conduct of the Abbey's ghosts only serves to emphasise one specifically dominant question - Why is Newstead Abbey, and places like it, so unique? What conspires to make it so *haunted*? Is it the site itself, or the people who have resided there? Or both?

Only the most stubborn and blinkered would ever deny the existence of the paranormal and, if further proof is needed, it will be discovered at Newstead Abbey...and beyond!

Any special awareness is opposed, and leads to unexpected conclusions.

'Alternative' communities inhabiting places like Newstead are not incarcerated against their will. Certain elements exist that are less accommodating, but only reflect on any host. Newstead generally exudes a warm, welcoming ambience quite different from the atmosphere generally perceived within haunted places.

The 'New Steade' was established in a clearing in forests that, even in mediaeval times, all but covered the County of Nottinghamshire. This is the same mighty forest of Sherwood through which Robin 'of the Hoode' is reputed to have roamed with purpose, the same forest that stretched almost to the gates of Nottingham itself. Significantly, adjacent to Newstead, lies a cave known as 'Robin Hood's Stable', and 'Robin's Chair' is located in the surrounding woods.

Whether these landmarks were used by this legendary figure is debatable, but used they were by people from much earlier times.

Implements fashioned by Neolithic man more than five thousand years ago have been discovered at nearby Bestwood. Mansfield, a mere five miles away, stands at the intersection of two Roman roads - Ryknield Street and Leeming Street (this latter still runs from Mansfield

Market Place) - and a Roman villa has been discovered at Mansfield Woodhouse. Unsurprising, therefore, that an ancient British brass spear head and other similar artifacts, along with Roman coins from the reigns of Vespasian, Constantius, Antonius Pius and Marcus Aurelius, the earliest of these dating back two-thousand five-hundred years, have been unearthed nearby.

Over the centuries Sherwood was gradually felled, the process accelerated during the 18th Century leaving little to compare with today.

Precisely when the land around Newstead became occupied is difficult to ascertain. Nottinghamshire had always been sparsely populated, reduced further in this area with its underlying Bunter Sandstone and free draining, impoverished topsoil, which made arable farming even more difficult. So in 1086 Newstead was not considered important enough to be even mentioned in the Domesday Book and is only first recorded in 1169. Small snatches of information do offer a tantalising glimpse into what may constitute its history.

The ancient British name for Nottingham was *Tigguocobaus*, meaning 'dwelling of caves', the early inhabitants of the County using natural caves in what became known as Castle Rock. This trait apparently lasted for centuries, with many of the Newstead employees living in similar cave dwellings until they were re-housed by either Thomas Wildman, or the Webbs. These Celtic ancestors probably belonged to a tribe known as *Brigantes* who lived in small, scattered hamlets close to a water source, clearing land for wheat and nurturing livestock. Thus a picture begins to form of these early Britons' way of life; of them clearing the ground around Newstead's caves, their practising of primitive agriculture, and their supplementation of diet with fish from the nearby River Leen.

Initially, these people worshipped pagan gods, but could have converted to Christianity as early as the 5th Century. This becomes inconsequential, for in subsequent centuries the area repeatedly changed hands; many of its invaders being Barbarians who only slowly relinquished the pagan practices they had imposed on the vanquished. In the 6th Century Angles came from northern Europe, the County thereafter forming a buffer zone between the competing rulers of Mercia and Northumbria. During this time the woods were hunted by Mercian kings who, in turn, granted privileges to favoured subjects.

Sherwood remained a Royal forest but sadly no documents detailing its use exist before the reign of Edward I (1272-1307).

In the 9th Century the Danes invaded, their 'Danelaw' holding sway. Gradually, they did accept the Christian faith only to have it usurped in the 10th Century by Olaf Guthfrithson, who re-invoked pagan rituals.

Doubtless the events had lasting influence on the site, and in cataloguing them we cannot overlook the various occupations, sometimes passive, more often brutal, for it is well-documented that these invaders possessed a casual attitude to violence and regularly used torture as a means of suppression. Christian worship would be a foreign, possibly subversive practice that warranted a few martyrdoms, alas unrecorded in this unexceptional place.

Why and when Newstead became a religious house is not known, although the Canons of Sherwood, as those occupants were called, did hold land as early as 1163. And we know that an early, wooden structure pre-dated the present stone buildings. Further, the siting of Christian establishments was rarely accidental. During the Dark Ages, in areas converted to Christianity by Rome's pioneering missionaries to Britain, pagan places of worship were often adopted by early Christian priests, partly because their converts already frequented them. Indeed, relics of pre-Christian pagan temples have been discovered in the County.

This supports the notion that Newstead's history begins centuries prior to it becoming a place of Christian worship and belief. So, what power drew those early devotees?

Constructed in close proximity to water-courses, such places of worship benefited from the energy said courses were believed to generate. Some were hidden and detected by dowsing or through use of the pendulum. This lends consideration to the ley line, of which one is said to pass through the site, thus promoting primitive affinity, the earth itself believed to be a source of power. If true, it is misleading to term the happenings at Newstead 'unearthly', since they are very much of the earth upon which the Abbey stands.

Early man worshipped various deities from the benign to dark, sinister gods, who demanded human sacrifice. Thankfully, such heinous practices have been subsequently moderated although their remnants still exist. In nearby Derbyshire, annual Well-Dressings have become a colourful celebration quite divorced from the original ceremonies in which the slaughtered body of a human being, or favourite animal, was cast into the waters to propitiate the gods and thus ensure a reliable supply of precious water.

Understandably, such customs will leave a marked impression on a site chosen for its particular characteristics, thereby forging definitive links with the supernatural.

In Newstead's grounds walk the Little White Lady and a phantom Cavalier. Ghostly hoof-beats and the wailing voice of the 5th Lord's sister reverberate. The strange shape of a monk appeared in a car's headlights as the vehicle negotiated Newstead's drive from the main Mansfield road. The driver, so scared by the sight, accelerated involuntarily into...and through the insubstantial shape!

Late one crisp, cold night a man who left the Abbey to walk towards Annesley passed the Waterfall where, to his horror, he saw a coach-and-four bearing wildly down upon him along the narrow drive. Self-preservation uppermost, the man flung himself into the cold water beneath the Fall. Clambering back out, soaked but unscathed, he was thankful to find the night as still and unsullied as when he had set out, but startled to discover that when he inspected the lane in both directions there was no coach, nor horses visible!

Could the coach have belonged to *Devil* Byron, - the very same coach into which he is reputed to have cast the murdered body of his coachman?

From the Pilgrim Oak, the centrepiece of many pagan-inspired rituals and festivities, Newstead bristles with such tales. Reports abound that some of the estate cottages are affected by ghostly voices, and filled with sounds reminiscent of boulders rolling across floors. Doors mysteriously open without use of visible hand.

Byron grasped the domain's ethereal qualities:

> *'But in the noontide of the moon, and when*
> *The wind is winged from one point of heaven,*
> *There moans a strange unearthly sound, which then*
> *Is musical - a dying accent driven.*
> *Through the huge arch, which soars and sinks again;*
> *Some deem it but the distant echo given*
> *Back to the night wind by the waterfall,*
> *And harmonised by the old choral wall.'*

One popular theory is that Newstead had been cursed by the ejected canons, in particular by one of their number who remains anonymous and who, steadfastly refusing to leave when Henry VIII's commissioners arrived, met a ghastly end. Furthermore, legend has it that the canons never relinquished their claim to the Priory and still maintain it to this day, even from their disturbed resting places.

Certainly this may be true, yet even so, were pagan priests removed by their Christian counterparts? If so, would they leave willingly, and relinquish *their* claim without seeking some form of retribution?

Maisie Hammond spoke of the tortured, soulful cries heard in the Prior's Oratory: *'It was a child, but so far back.'* If there is any relevance here, that pathetic child met its end many years before the Priory's demise, and many more before the canons would utter their curse.

We are aware that barbarous practices were carried out by the less pious brethren. Therefore, to what other deity would their victims appeal for succour, and vengeance, their pitiful souls having been so disabused of their faith?

Perhaps the answer *is* far more complicated.

An accumulation of events and personalities have added to the influences and fashioned the Abbey into an instrument capable of transgressing, even transposing time, circumstances relevant to countless similar places throughout the United Kingdom, indeed world-wide.

There is, however, one added ingredient that makes Newstead more unusual. It is the presence of a very special mind - that of the poet Byron, with his very particular, sometimes enigmatic capabilities. To quote R.W. Emerson: 'Perhaps there are men whose magnetisms are of that force to draw material and elemental powers, and, where they appear, immense instrumentalities organise around them.'

III

"So, what am I?" Byron again poses *the* question as he glances towards the doorway and his nemesis. "Am I corporeal, or as insubstantial as the mist gathering on the lake? Am I the briefest of utterances, a name mentioned, then as quickly forgotten? Or..." His tone takes on a more sinister implication. "Or am I an infrequent disclosure of some dreadful secret so vile it may only be hinted at?"

"Possibly." The reply retains that certain quality hinted at by Byron, a darkness still evident. "But you must consider, my lord, that you are a poet and so a conjurer who will perform on a public stage. You yourself wrote: *'What is Poetry? The feeling of a Former world and Future.'*

"Do not writers inhabit a shifting landscape populated by created shades which are further enhanced in the minds of readers?"

A silence prevails as Byron contemplates the significance of this. He reflects that like Newstead's phantoms, these created forms will hide behind a transparent veil, glimpsed but infuriatingly remain beyond reach.

In attempting to depict these shapes as thoughts on paper, consider what kind of mind takes a plethora of words and proceeds to re-arrange them into a form, which hopefully, evokes the most sublime images.

Poetry is largely autobiographical, perhaps more than in any other form of writing. It calls upon past experiences, using them to create concepts which sometimes influence the future. Certain creations, specifically those connecting innermost thoughts and sensations, gain a life of their own, and cease being mere words. More, they are dreams often as substantial or insubstantial as ourselves, which can, and do, become reality.

Like Mary Shelley's *Frankenstein*, the writer, and her fictional *alter-ego*, the Baron, conceived a living creature, one which quickly slips from the Baron's grasp.

Slips from his grasp!

Vampires. Imagination. Or something far more inexplicable, more terrifying? Byron tired of his creation a short time after that storm-filled night at the Villa

Diodati, but by then it had assumed a life of its own and refused to die. In a sense it becomes self-perpetuating and will always encapsulate man's darkest, most fundamental dread.

Here we arrive at the crux, as did Byron's own creation *Manfred*. Man - half deity, half dust - is most troubled by the spirits he invokes, and we, like Manfred, are convulsed, seeking things beyond mortality.

"So, must *I* bear the blame?" Challenges Byron.

"You must bear nothing, except that which your own conscience demands," the voice states. "And responsibility for those phantoms given life by your word and deed."

Byron retaliates. "Oh. And which came first?" He reflects on the source of his ideas whose very essence seethes within the walls of this, his home. A spiralling column of chilling vapour; a dark entity which oozes from floors; shadows forming suggestive shapes as they flit across darkened rooms, there and gone - in a blink. Seen, yet not seen. Imagination? Or reality? Or perhaps more edifying, only seen when *they* wished it.

"Such creativity is possessed by few," the voice continues. "Accept that your place is *here*, for here you can never die."

Byron argues, "It is not the place *I* chose." His final orders to Doctor Millingen come to mind: '...*here let my bones moulder...*'

"You flatter yourself, poet, if you consider that the choice was ever yours. There is something else you must know. To understand this, we must make a journey..."

The high vaulted ceiling of Hucknall church absorbs the scraping and digging sounds as men labour under instruction.

"Today," Byron is told, "is Wednesday 15th June, 1938. Hark ye and look, my lord, all will be revealed."

As the church clock has recently chimed five, the desultory tone is interrupted by the grunts of the labourers as they struggle to lift a large flagstone situated where once had been the Chancel steps.

THE HIDDEN FACE OF DESTINY

Following more long minutes of labour, the stone is laid aside revealing eleven stone steps descending in an easterly direction, each step three feet nine inches in width and eight inches in height.

"Follow, Lord Byron, look close, discover destiny."

Byron hesitates, uncertain, perhaps afraid.

After a further brief inspection the men involved in the task depart, the church left silent, the echo of its door closing dissipating, swallowed into silence.

At a gesture from the figure, Byron descends into the claustrophobic vault onto a floor littered with debris, shadowed confines stacked with coffins.

At the foot of a small coffin lies a chest whose faded purple velvet cover is only evidenced by a few tatty remnants. It stands upright on its smaller end, its body adorned with brass headed nails and brass funerary ornaments.

Byron gasps as he leans forward to read the brass plate screwed to the lid.

"Within this Urn
are deposited
the heart and the brain
of the deceased
Lord Noel Byron."

The poet recoils, stumbles to the wall, reliant on its support. Disbelief scours his face, eyes probing the shadows seeking succour from his companion.

The coronet on the lid of the oak coffin, still in a remarkable state of preservation, mocks Byron for he recognises it. But gone are its six pearls and its cap of crimson velvet lined with ermine. Nor is there a plate screwed to the coffin, that too having been removed.

"Draw nearer, good lord, for you must see." Another inviting gesture.

Byron, more nervous now, reluctantly obeys. The box lid is loose, and slides to one side to reveal an inner sleeve of wood. The lid is raised and he staggers a little as he looks upon the embalmed body lying there, its features still recognisable. It wears a serene, almost happy expression, the hair easily distinguished from portraits and mirrors.

He looks upon himself.

"Enough!" Byron staggers away only to stumble into his daughter, Ada's coffin. He catches sight of lines inscribed on a plate and recites in part... "'Augusta Ada...only daughter of George Gordon Noel Lord Byron...Born 10th December 1815. Died 27th November 1852.'"

Instantly, he recalls the cries of pain heard in the Oratory, the very fact of him almost pulling a pistol. "Dead! All dead," he cries.

In answer, the form recites:

"'And when, at length, the mind shall be all free
From what it hates in this degraded form,
Reft of its carnal life, save what shall be
Existent happier in the fly and worm -
When elements to elements conform,
And dust is as it should be, shall I not
Feel all I see, less dazzling, but more warm?
The bodiless thought? the Spirit of each spot?
Of which, even now, I share at times the immortal lot?'"

"Why taunt me this way?"
"In order that you recognise the lines, good sir?"
"Surely so, I penned them."

"Then it proved prophetic." The figure beckons again. "It is time to leave."

"One moment, shade, tell me, if that is me lying asleep then how come I am here?"

"Having arrived and also seen proof, why do you so readily forget the journey? You have already walked this path, yet I see we must travel it once more."

An exasperated sigh steals through the air.

"Do you, Lord Byron, recollect how in your youth, you addressed the concept of mortality, in your view at that time the inevitable conclusion to existence?

"In September 1811 you sent two letters to Frances Hodgson. In the first, dated the 3rd September, you wrote: *'I will have nothing to do with your immortality...'*"

Byron interrupts, takes up the quote: "*'...we are miserable enough in this life, without the absurdity of speculating upon another. If men are to live, why die at all? and if they die, why disturb the sweet and sound sleep that "knows no waking"? There is nothing after death and death is itself nothing.'*" Byron concludes by stating: "It's a quotation from Seneca.

"And on the 13th, I wrote: *'...And our carcasses, which are to rise again, are they worth raising? I hope, if mine is, I hope that I shall have a better* pair of legs.*'*

The figure comments: "A somewhat droll insight if I might be permitted to say. Yet, as the years passed, you began to differentiate physical being from some indestructible element that survived death. In one of your light-hearted moods you sent a missive to Thomas Moore on the 11th April 1817 in which you said: *'One certainly has a soul; but how it came to allow itself to be enclosed in a body is more than I can imagine. I only know if once mine gets out, I'll have a bit of a tussle before I let it get in again to that or any other. "'*

Byron shakes his head slowly, a slight upturn of lips evident. The other continues: "Must I remind you of your thinking barely five years later?"

"Certainly," Byron says, "my thinking had become more focussed and profound. This I believe you will find in my 'Letters and Journals': *'Of the Immortality of the Soul, it appears to me that there can be little doubt...that the* Mind *is* eternal, *seems as probable as that the body is not so. "'*

He contemplates the figure. "You should know that I refuse to subscribe to orthodox religious views, preferring instead to come to my own accommodation. I have always acknowledged the philosophy of even the most committed atheist or agnostic such as I has been shaped by his early upbringing under some religious influence or other. It seems impossible to consider the afterlife without using religious concepts, and vocabulary. I regret I am no exception.

"I was, it seems justifiably, convinced of the continued existence of something vital within me which would transcend death. Thank yourself for this," he adds addressing his companion, "it was those first, tantalising glimpses you permitted which sowed the seeds of my conviction; our brief confrontations in those dark, melancholy months which helped shape this insight."

Byron brushes past the figure, aware only of a shift of air, of nothing substantial. Stooping, he comes up the steps and away from that malodorous vault, to drink in the cold, damp smell of the church, but one which is far more appetising than the one below.

He looks up at the stained glass window. "So," he eventually says, "have we completed our journey? Am I as altered as the ancestral home about which I am forced to wander? Strangely, I do not know the means by which I have travelled."

"Move on," the voice impresses, "to 1822 and to what is contained in your journal, 'Detached Thoughts'. *Matter is eternal, always changing, but reproduced, and, as far as we can comprehend Eternity Eternal; and why not* Mind? *Why should not the Mind act with and upon the Universe?*'"

Byron sinks onto a pew to gaze steadily at the cloaked figure. "It appears then that Mind is the fundamental mechanism after all. But whose mind? Is it all enacted in our own mind, that being 'real' to us? Are we nothing but dreams, simply reality transposed to another plane?

"May I quote this?

"'Our life is two-fold: Sleep hath its own world,
A boundary between the things misnamed
Death and existence: Sleep hath its own world,
And a wide realm of wild reality.
And dreams in their development have breath,
And tears, and tortures, and the touch of joy;
They leave a weight upon our waking thoughts,
They take a weight from off our waking toils,
They do divide our being; they become
A portion of ourselves as of our time,
And look like heralds of eternity;

They pass like spirits of the past, - they speak
Like Sibyls of the future; they have power -
The tyranny of pleasure and of pain;
They make us what we were not - what they will,
And shake us with the vision that's gone by,
The dread of vanish'd shadows - Are they so?
Is not the past all shadow? - What are they?
Creations of the mind? - The mind can make
Substance, and people planets of its own
With beings brighter than have been, and give
A breath to forms which can outlive all flesh.'

"I believe, whoever you are," Byron concludes, "that this verse, *my* verse states all." He does not require an answer for what has been said, or done. He falls into silent contemplation considering that if our minds are infiltrated, our thoughts supplanted with that of another - then surely that other mind must be at work on us and our surroundings.

More than a century later, this anticipation of ideas which science was only just beginning to grapple with, is breathtaking. Writing in 1927, Sir Arthur Eddington admitted: 'The stuff of the world is mind stuff.' And in 1931, Sir James Jeans wrote: '...the universe begins to look more like a great thought than a great machine.'
Added to the already lengthy list of coincidences touching the Abbey, the point is passed where the only possible operative agency is more than mere chance.
"What then is reality?" Byron wonders. He looks up. "Friend, is that the answer? Could some cerebral element

attach itself to a place, creating these ghosts...good or bad? Are we all pawns in some dark strategy?"

Air curls, grows thicker, a gesture of annoyance imprisoned within it. "Friend! You presume too much, sir, if you address me as 'friend'. If such strategy exists it is there to be learned, hardly revealed. Learned, and accepted for what it is. You, my lord, understand the nature of things, more so now. You should hold the courage of your convictions!" A sigh? A laugh? eddies, somehow disdainful, sarcastic in its implication. "Hear then another quotation of your own: *"The mind which is immortal makes itself requital for its good or evil thoughts - is its own origin of ill and end -'.*

"How little you differ from the stones that surround you, poet ."

"Think on this," Byron interjects angrily. *"'I live not in myself, but I become a portion of that around me.'* And also, *'Are not the mountains, waves, and skies, a part of me and of my soul, as I of them?'"*

"Oh yes, the proud poet...the *Lord Poet*. By your very recital you acknowledge what I say. You hardly differ from the surrounding stones, nor are you any more than a small disturbance on an ocean of energy. Yes, my lord, everything around us is as insubstantial as dreams...to more or less quote yourself!

"So, of you and the stones, which of you lives? There is, most assuredly, a strategy, of which we are all a part. "Therefore should you not have asked: *'Why should not the mind act with and upon darkness for **She was the universe'**?"*

The words bulge the very fabric of the church, clouds form, dissipate then reform, thunder heads scowl, issue muted laughter... fade into the slow, solemn beat of a drum...Into the shrouded form by his bedside, the blood-sucking leeches. And he reaches to touch...grab...tear away...

"We must capture the soul," states one surgeon.

Byron silently screams: *'I knew, and know my hour is come, but not to render up my soul to such as thee.'*

They shall not dissect his body, or search for his very essence...But it is, even now, too late...

Byron's shaking hands tear at the cowl, tear it aside to reveal...*Himself!*

'He unveils his aspect: on his brow the thunder-scars are graven; from his eye glares forth the immortality of hell.'

An echo: the voice again, still here: *'"The genius of this mortal, - Come! 'Tis time."'*

He gives up the ghost.

And in Missolonghi the cry stains the air: *"BYRON IS DEAD."*

CHAPTER ELEVEN

FINAL VERSE

--oOo--

Could Lord Byron have anticipated the truth?

Does something exist within Newstead Abbey that we can only dimly recognise?

It holds many secrets, some of which will surely throw light on these intriguing issues. Also contained within them is the strategy for survival. Moreover, there is a lingering suspicion that all of us are already, or will *become*, through whatever lives we lead, a part of that strategy.

The experiences of the Abbey's personnel underline how Newstead has managed to extend its influence well beyond its own physical confines. And that Byron has truly played his part in its survival.

We must also conclude that of all those who might have acquired Newstead Abbey from the desperately impoverished poet, his friend and successor Thomas Wildman, donated both fortune and health towards its survival, thus creating a shrine to his illustrious school-friend.

After her visit to Newstead in September 1850, Byron's daughter Ada, wrote of Wildman: 'It has been the *salvation* of Newstead, that he has had it. No one else in the world could have *resuscitated* it, & all its *best* reminiscences, as *he* has done.'

Wildman's successors have, in their turn, added to that legacy.

Is it therefore possible to discount that we are, albeit unwittingly, a part of that plan?

Consider what drew us to Newstead Abbey, constrained us to write about the place and its residents, past and present, and how they directed and ultimately influenced our research.

Similarly, readers should perhaps examine what induced their selection of this book.

Above all, they should consider what persuaded us to end this account with the following lines, penned by the poet on leaving Newstead, a place of shadows, the only place where perhaps his heart belongs.

'Haply, thy sun, emerging, yet may shine,
Thee to irradiate with meridian ray;
Hours splendid as the past may still be thine,
And bless thy future, as thy former day.'

This is the most chilling thought of all.

PUBLISHERS' NOTE:
FORTHCOMING BOOK ABOUT LORD BYRON

"SINISTER QUARTET - BYRON, SHELLEY AND THE VILLA DIODATI"

If you enjoyed this book, look out for the next masterpiece. An enthralling story about Byron, the Shelleys, a young, jealous and evil Doctor John Polidori and the Villa Diodati - a sinister place where we meet them on a fearful night in June, 1816, when this dark quartet are trapped by a terrible storm.

In the half-light of the Villa Diodati four people debate the nature of life and death. Lightning torches the peaks of the Jura mountains, power is unleashed - mental and physical - each of the gathering already acutely aware of his or her own mortality and all anxious to learn what might lie beyond the pale.

RAISING THE DEAD

Ghost stories abound precipitating speculation, and harmless exhortation resulting in the promotion of the abhorrent emergence of man's basest fears - horror that will ultimately haunt humankind and eventually consume the Quartet's own true selves.

Pure evil is created through the imagination of Literary icons Byron and Mary Shelley - The Vampyre, a being who defeats death and a creature created from the dead - an evil that blurs the distinction between Heaven and Hell. This book lends originality and insight to the exploration into the human psyche by examining the borderline where imagination and reality overlap.

--oOo--

Another spectacular book by Derek Fox

REVIEWS OF DEREK FOX'S PREVIOUS WORK

Mark Chadbourn - Fantasy Author:
'Derek Fox is set to be a new master of fear'

Mick Simms Editor/Publisher
'A fine writer with a subtle technique that blends horror with the poetic.'

Paul Ward - Reviewer
Horror Writers' Assoc'n USA, on 'Treading on the Past':
'With production values that are superb, professional illustrations and D.M. Fox writing it, it is difficult to imagine a production that would not ooze quality.'

Two on short story 'Porcelain' in the Britiah Fantasy Society Anthology F20

Ellen Datlow - New York, Editor 'The Year's Best Horror'

'A story worthy of inclusion in my Honourable Mention List and also in my summary in the book.'

William P Simmons for 'Horror.Net' USA (on 'Porcelain')

'Told in hues of light and shadow, this story is remarkable in its ability to physically reflect the inner anguish of its characters, whispering everything, giving away nothing.'